100 Years of Canadian Drawings

Other books by the author

On the Enjoyment of Modern Art
Canadian, U.S. and German Editions

The Nude in Canadian Painting

Canadian Artists and Airmen, 1940–45

Adrift on Course
Memoir illustrated by the author

100 Years of Canadian Drawings

Jerrold Morris

⑪ Methuen
Toronto New York London Sydney

Cover design–Gerry Gauthier

Cover illustration, detail of *Self-Portrait* by
Gordon Rayner. Complete drawing is reproduced on page 141.

Canadian Cataloguing in Publication Data

Morris, Jerrold, 1911-
    One hundred years of Canadian drawings

ISBN 0-458-94570-6

1. Drawing, Canadian.   2. Drawing–19th century–
Canada.   3. Drawing–20th century–Canada.

I. Title.

NC141.M67   741.971   C80-094506-9

Printed and bound in Canada
1 2 3 4 5   80   4 3 2 1 0

Contents

Acknowledgments

I should like to express my thanks to the artists, collectors, museums and public and commercial art galleries who have assisted in the compilation of this anthology. In particular: Mimi Cazort of the National Gallery of Canada, Dennis Reid, Catherine Lochnan and Sybille Pantazzi of the Art Gallery of Ontario, Dr. Micheline Moisan of the Montreal Museum of Fine Arts, Francis K. Smith of the Agnes Etherington Art Centre, Paul Bennett of Gallery/Stratford, Chris Varley of the Edmonton Art Gallery and Joan Murray of the Robert McLaughlin Gallery, Oshawa.

"... the worship of images, my great, my sole, my primeval passion"
Baudelaire

Introduction

This book is an anthology of one hundred years of Canadian drawings. To do justice to any one artist included was not easy, and it should also be borne in mind that the particular examples I have selected represent only one phase or one period of an artist's work. Finding material was difficult and my problems were compounded by the vastness of this country; my search not only was time-consuming but left me with a relentlessly nagging suspicion that many more undiscovered drawings were lurking in obscure places. To cite one example, after years of enquiry I have failed to locate works by those women artists who together with Edwin Holgate formed the Beaver Hall group in Montreal.

The idea for *One Hundred Years of Canadian Drawings* began some years ago when I wanted to write a one-volume book on Canadian drawings, including those from the Colonial period. In the course of my research I extensively toured the country, visiting most of our art museums and provincial archives. Eventually, I decided to abandon the project, having concluded that such a wide perspective could not be dealt with effectively in one volume.

When in the summer of 1979, Gallery/Stratford invited me to organize an exhibition of twentieth century Canadian drawings to be shown during the Festival season, it occurred to me that the work for this exhibition might form the nucleus of the modern section for the book I had wanted to write long ago.

This, then, is my own personal best effort after many years of digging. It is intended to contribute to the appreciation of drawings, which have only recently attracted much attention in Canada. Part of the blame for this neglect is due to the lack of leadership offered by our art institutions which, with very few exceptions, have gathered only the skimpiest drawing collections; and even the most exceptional are of necessity often stored in areas inaccessible to the public.

It is unfortunate that many people continue to regard drawing as a minor art form, at best a preparatory stage for elaboration in another medium. Even when this is the case, it is possible to enjoy the particular delight of drawing in its own right; more often than not the drawings presented here were made by an artist as independent works.

Selection involves the critical process, and I should state at the outset what my criteria were. Every work of art should be assessed on its own terms—the artist's intent, the resources he or she commands (talent and developed skills) and the success of his or her achievement in a chosen medium. By these standards a very wide range of art can be enjoyed, from the naive to the products of genius. Once one has defined the limitations, one can even obtain pleasure from some academic works.

The lover of drawings has the advantage of being in close contact with the artist's original concept conveyed in a relatively uncomplicated medium. Drawing, in the widest sense of the term, is the linear element in art least susceptible to manipulation by what Blake called "Blotting" and the Pre-Raphaelites called "Slosh"—we might call it "fudging." Among painters are many masters of camouflage, what Ingres meant when he said that drawing is "the probity of art."

Another advantage is that in our appreciation of drawings we are not involved in the tiresome search for the "important" work—which is not unconnected with scale. We can accept, and enjoy, very small statements on paper which would be thought to be totally inconsequential on canvas.

More important is the fact that we do not have to concern ourselves with trends or fashions. The art of the West, or "international" art, has been driven in this century to renew itself in change by reacting against what immediately preceded it. This process has been accelerated by the pressure exerted by art-watchers, particularly formalist critics, who not long ago had arrived at the position that painting should confine itself to the exercise of color dynamics on a two-dimensional plane (preserved in its "integrity"), eschewing all content which might be deemed the preserve of other media. They even proposed an acceptable way of laying on paint—the word went out to thin it down.

Fortunately these narrow pundits are in retreat before the forces of diversity. But there is no doubt that many artists felt threatened by them. However, in the graphic media they remained free to express themselves at will.

Though modified by modern sensibilities, the art of drawing retains its traditional virtues. No one can criticize an artist for drawing something concrete. One has only to think of Harold Town who, while pursuing his development as a Non-Objective painter, has continued to be the most prolific figurative draughtsman in the country.

A whole range of Non-Objective drawings, of the kind in which the artist is pre-occupied with purely formal considerations, has been attempted. Because this book is intended as a celebration of the endless fascination of images, such works are not included here.

I have chosen to begin my story in 1880, the year when the number of professional artists in Canada had grown to the point where the formation of a National Academy had not only become desirable but necessary. It was also the year in which the National Gallery of Canada was founded.

As some kind of structure was essential, the book is in chronological order—at least in relation to movements, if not always to individuals.

Prelude to 1880:
The Colonial Period

During the Colonial period the pictorial record was largely the work of artists who were neither native-born nor immigrants, but transients.

The majority were army officers who had been trained at military establishments such as Woolwich, where the English watercolor painter Paul Sandby was drawing instructor. There is a rich store of this material in the various archives across the land, much of it unpublished.

By the mid-nineteenth century this record was amplified by immigrants whose work was not only directed to a European public avid for information about North America, but also to a local public served by various illustrated publications.

Much of their work was achieved in the watercolor medium because of its suitability for on-the-spot reporting and ready transformation into prints or magazine illustrations.

Typical of these elaborated drawings is the example of John Henry Walker (Pl. 1), who emigrated to Canada in 1842 and worked for the *Canadian Illustrated News* and other publications.

1. **John Henry Walker** (1831–1899)
Ruins of the Roman Catholic Bishop's Palace,
Montreal, c.1854. Ink and watercolor, 10¼ x
15¼ ins (26.1 x 38.7 cm). Collection: The
McCord Museum, Montreal.

The subject matter favored by artists in colonial times ranged from coastal scenes, townscapes and landscapes to vignettes of garrison, native and settlement life and, increasingly as time went by, to westward exploration.

In Quebec the early emphasis was on portraiture and religious paintings. Baillargé was one of the first native-born artists to set up a studio in Quebec. After study in Paris from 1778 to 1781 he practiced as a sculptor, architect and painter. His study (Pl. 2) is typical of the Baroque style common to most religious works in French Canada. Such a painting may be seen on the church wall in Huot's drawing (Pl. 41).

Because so much of the art produced in the colonial period was "for the record" it tends to lack vitality; its value is largely historical. More provocative is the work of untrained artists whose vision was not shaped by preconceived notions learned in the schools. Four examples will suffice.

The anonymous drawing of garrison troops in Quebec (Pl. 3) betrays a lack of technical skill and a want of understanding of the laws of perspective. The figures are stiffly drawn in a childlike manner and a ruler has been used as an aid in depicting the buildings. Nevertheless we have the impression of a lively scene viewed through

2. **François Baillargé** (1759–1830)
L'Ange Gardien. Ink with watercolor,
11½ x 9⅞ ins (29.2 x 25 cm).
Collection: Musée du Québec.

an oval aperture completed at the top by the clouds. Indeed the whole has the appearance of a theatre set, with the troops disappearing off stage right. The presentation is very convincing despite the lack of professional skill.

3. Anonymous
The Quebec Volunteers, Palace Gate. Ink, 12¾ x 10¼ ins (32.4 x 26 cm). Collection: Musée du Québec.

Just as convincing is the drawing of York boats by George Finlay (Pl. 4). No amount of sophistication could have added to the vividness of the impression conveyed by this simple depiction of the event.

4. George E. Finlay (Active 1837–48)
Two York Boats Passing En Route, 1846. Ink, 3¼ x 10 ins (8.3 x 10.3 cm). Collection: The Glenbow–Alberta Institute, Calgary.

In the Quebec garrison scene and the drawing of York boats one has the impression that the artist has witnessed the occasion and is making a record of it, but Baxter's drawing of the Indian Chief's daughter (Pl. 5) is probably a product of the imagination. Her accoutrements may be taken from life, but the girl has more the appearance of a figure in a pantomime than a real-life Indian.

Many of the artists who made journeys to the West to record native life were inclined to present Indians as an exotic compendium to the landscape, formulae as little differentiated as the trees. Even in the case of the portraits one gets the impression that many of them were done by rote. But in the Baxter drawing we catch an echo of the legendary Pocahantas, who was received in England as a princess in 1616. It reflects the nineteenth century romantic view of Indians typified in such works as Chateaubriand's *Atala* published in 1801 with illustrations by Gustave Doré, or Longfellow's *The Song of Hiawatha* of 1855.

Possibly between the presentation of native people as exotic adjuncts to landscape and their treatment as subjects for romantic literature lies our failure to come to terms with them in the land we now all share. Emily Carr long ago, in spite of her upbringing and the social prejudices of the time, found nothing untoward in her relationship with them. (See Pl. 101).

5. **Dudley Baxter**
Portrait of an Indian Chief's Daughter.
Ink with watercolor, 6¾ x 4¾ ins (17.1 x 12 cm). Collection: Musée du Québec.

Like the Indians, the habitants of Quebec were molded into stereotypes by Krieghoff in mid-century. If we want to view them as other than rolly-polly figures of fun in the manner of Brueghel we can again turn to the work of amateurs.

In Crawford Young's drawing (Pl. 6) we find the familiar pipes and clothing, but the men are depicted as individuals of dignified mien.

6. **J. Crawford Young** (Active 1825–36)
Canadian Habitants. Ink with watercolor, 9½ x 10 ins (24.1 x 25.4 cm). Collection: The McCord Museum, Montreal.

The Academic Era

The Royal Canadian Academy was founded in 1880 under the patronage of the Governor General, the Marquis of Lorne.

The aims of its founders were the same as those which prompted the establishment in 1768 of the Royal Academy in England in the reign of George III—to maintain professional standards, raise the social status of artists, facilitate a wider dissemination of their work, and hence improve their marketing prospects.

At its inception the Royal Academy in England numbered among its members most of the finest artists of the day: Reynolds was its first President. Although there were later defections, it continued to be an influential body until the early years of the twentieth century. The same situation existed in Canada a century later. The first President of the Royal Canadian Academy was Lucius O'Brien, and the charter members included the majority of Canada's most highly regarded artists.

The designation "academic" as used here does not imply that all the artists whose work we shall be considering were members of the Academy. It is used to describe the kind of art prescribed or found to be acceptable by academies everywhere—that is to say "official" art.

The character of official art in nineteenth century Europe was largely determined by the Establishment and various levels of government. Of great importance were exhibitions organized by the Royal Academy and the Paris Salon. Because artists depend on patronage for their livelihood, it was of vital interest that they be able to gain admission to these exhibitions: thus art politics had its inception. While the academies were supportive of artists they approved of, they were also restrictive, resisting any changes which might undermine their authority to guide public taste, which was largely molded by the productions of their members.

As André Malraux wrote in *Voices of Silence*:

> If the subjects of the official Salon artists are meretricious, this is because, far from being conjured up by the art of those who painted them, they are models to which this art submits itself.

The struggle to open the doors of official tribunals became the driving force of nineteenth century revolutionary activity by artists. In Paris the breakthrough came in 1863 when Napoleon III, in response to pressure from artists excluded from the official Salon, set up the Salon des Refusés. This was followed by the organization of the Salon des Indépendants in 1884.

By the end of the century this battle had been won, but in the meantime many artists had suffered hardships at the hands of exclusive juries. All too often private collectors showed more discrimination than did official bodies. While the Musée du Luxembourg, owing to indignant protest from the Institut, was refusing to accept seventeen canvases from the Caillebotte bequest (including works by Renoir, Sisley, Cézanne and Manet), individuals such as the Russians Tschoukine and Morosov were acquiring masterpieces which finally enriched the Hermitage Museum in Moscow, and Americans in Paris were buying the French paintings which are the pride of their country's museums today.

In Canada progress toward freedom of expression was delayed for a generation. The Academic Era dragged on long after the opening of the twentieth century. Indeed it was not until after the First World War that any significant awakening can be detected in Canadian art to the climactic changes which had taken place in Europe since Impressionism.

The great innovators of the nineteenth

century have been thoroughly investigated. No one as yet seems to have tried to find in the works of the academicians those qualities which can be appreciated in the light of contemporary taste. Because the best Canadian artists of the period, corseted by popular taste, were guided into conservative channels, we may expect to detect their true talents in works never intended for public exhibition.

Some years ago I planned an exhibition to explore this thesis by confronting a selection of their showpieces with a sampling of drawings and preparatory sketches—catching them unawares so to speak! On this project I received a letter from the English art critic, Eric Newton, from which I quote:

This seems to me a most fruitful line of research. I am convinced that you are right in thinking that the cloud that hangs over academic painting today is by no means justified and that many of the qualities which have brought it into disrepute with modern critics have been imposed on the academicians by outside influences rather than evolved by the artists themselves as a result of their own lack of sensitivity or creative imagination.

I hope that in some small degree the drawings reproduced in this book may further future research in the area.

R.C.A.–Some Charter Members

While drawings of the Colonial period abound, those of the last decades of the nineteenth century are hard to come by.

A flourishing school of painters in watercolor existed during this period, but their works can hardly qualify for inclusion in this book. In a few cases I have stretched a point in order to represent an artist by selecting a work on paper which might be described as a drawing enhanced by watercolor.

The dearth of drawings of the 1880s and 1890s may be explained by the fact they were regarded, if at all, as preparatory studies for paintings, and therefore are to be found mostly in sketchbooks, few of which have survived.

The drawings I have been able to trace by charter members of the R.C.A. and their contemporaries reflect in some measure the preoccupation of artists at the time. Landscape remained a primary concern, followed by subjects dealing with current events and everyday life, in the home or on the farms. Portraits continued to be in demand along with religious paintings, and a few historical and "fancy" pictures. Increasingly, Western subject matter became popular.

The main difference between the art produced in this period and that of Colonial times is its increased professionalism, brought about by emigration of artists to Canada and the large number of native-born artists who had studied abroad. Of the charter members represented here, six were immigrants.

Study abroad had greatly diversified the sources of influence on Canadian art. In the Colonial period these were largely derived from England, but now Paris influence predominated, with some contribution from the Dutch School of the Hague and the American Hudson River School.

Lucius O'Brien
1832–1899

O'Brien was the first President of the R.C.A. and one of the first artists to paint in the far west. He was art editor of *Picturesque Canada*, published in 1882.

Affected by the rage of the time for the sublime and the picturesque, he evidently fell under the spell of one of its most prominent practitioners, the American Albert Bierstadt.

In this rare drawing we can detect O'Brien's concern with light which is so apparent in his diploma work "Sunrise on the Saguenay."

A group of artists, most of them Americans, who employed a pervasive atmospheric source of light in their paintings to engender a transcendent quality, were known as "Luminists."

7. **Lucius O'Brien**
Intshekoi, British Columbia,
1898. Ink over pencil, 9¼ x 8 ins
(23.6 x 20.2 cm). Collection: The
Ontario College of Art.

Daniel Fowler
1810–1894

Fowler was a watercolor painter and a founding member of the Ontario Society of Artists in 1872, which is the date of our drawing.

It reflects the continuing interest in genre subjects. In its Germanic attention to detail it probably draws on the experiences of his European tour in the 1830s.

8. Daniel Fowler
Man in Doorway, Smoking,
1872. Ink, 10¾ x 9½ ins
(27.3 x 24 cm). Collection: The
Montreal Museum of Fine
Arts. Gift of Miss Beryl
Wilson, 1948.

George Harlow White
1817–1887

9. George Harlow White
Study of Children, 1879. Ink with watercolor,
7 x 5¼ ins (17.8 x 13.3 cm). Private collection,
Toronto.

White was in Canada from 1871 until 1877 when he returned to England. He travelled extensively in Canada. It is a matter of some interest that he became a charter member of the R.C.A. after he had left the country and that his diploma picture was a landscape painted in Wales.

It is not generally realized that a large proportion of the works entered in exhibitions in Canada in the latter part of the nineteenth century, including those of the R.C.A., were of British subject matter. White continued to send pictures back to Canada after he had returned to England. Our drawing of children (Pl. 9) is one of these, and another example of the genre subjects beloved of the Victorians.

He was a meticulous draughtsman and, as may be seen in the Quebec landscape (Pl. 10), was inclined to select picturesque subjects pleasing to contemporary taste.

10. George Harlow White
The Forest, Canada: Rocks and Trees, Quebec, 1876. Pencil, 6½ x 4¾ ins (16.5 x 12 cm). Collection: The Agnes Etherington Art Centre, Queen's University, Kingston.

Napoléon Bourassa
1827–1916

An alternative to the all-pervasive Baroque style in religious painting in Quebec was the Neo-Classical style of the late eighteenth century exemplified by the French master Jacques-Louis David.

After studying with Théophile Hamel in Quebec, Bourassa went for further instruction to Florence and Rome where he came under the influence of Overbeck, one of the quasi-religious communities of German artists calling themselves the "Nazarines." Like David, they admired the work of John Flaxman (1755–1826). It is therefore possible to trace the source of our drawing back to England in the eighteenth century.

11. Napoléon Bourassa
Promesse de Rédemption. Detail: *Adam et Eve.*
Pencil heightened with white chalk, 12⅜ x 17⅞ ins
(**31.4 x 45.4 cm**). Collection: Musée du Québec.

William Raphael
1833–1914

Raphael was active in Montreal where he was a member of the Society of Canadian Artists in 1867.

One of his best known paintings is "Immigrants at Montreal" in the collection of the National Gallery of Canada. It was probably for just such a canvas with its crowd scene that our study was made. It has all the immediacy and illumination of a snapshot and is a beautiful example of my thesis that the talent of the academicians is to be discovered in their drawings. This one has the authority of a note by a Renaissance master.

12. William Raphael
Page from a Sketchbook, 1881–3. Graphite, 4¾ x 7 ins (12.1 x 17.8 cm). Collection: The McCord Museum, Montreal.

John A. Fraser
1838–1898

Fraser studied at the Royal Academy Schools in London and came to Canada in 1856. Subsequently he became a partner in the Notman firm. He was employed to paint the Rocky Mountains for the C.P.R.

One can see from this drawing how all local activity was centered on the railway. The sweep of the panorama is remarkable when one considers the small size of the sketchbook.

13. John A. Fraser
Medicine Hat, 1883. Pencil heightened with white.
Page size 4⅜ x 8½ ins (11.1 x 21.6 cm).
Collection: Mrs. Joan S. Muller, Bakersfield, U.S.A.

T. Mower Martin
1838–1934

After the issuing of free passes to artists by the
C.P.R., Martin, with F. M. Bell-Smith, Lucius
O'Brien and Marmaduke Matthews, first visited
the Rockies in 1887. He returned many times.

Our example of his work probably repre-
sents a mining camp, with the Rockies in the
background.

14. T. Mower Martin
Log Cabins, Western Canada, 1898. Pencil with
watercolor, 12½ x 19 ins (31.8 x 48.3 cm).
Private collection, Toronto.

John Henry Sandham
1842–1910

This drawing can be categorized as a "history picture," relating the story of the rescue of survivors from an abortive settlement attempt by the French from 1598 to 1603.

The history picture, representing actual or mythological events, was considered in the eighteenth century to be the most worthy subject for the attention of academicians. By the nineteenth century it was superseded by the depiction of current events.

Sandham's drawing may have been a study for an illustration in some periodical.

15. **John Henry Sandham**
Sable Island, A.D. 1603. Pencil, 9½ x 5⅜ ins (24.1 x 13.7 cm). Collection: The Montreal Museum of Fine Arts. Gift of George Iles, 1918.

Allan Edson
1846–1888

Like William Raphael (see Pl. 12), Edson was a founding member of the Society of Canadian Artists in Montreal.

He made several trips to Europe and these two pages from a sketchbook were undoubtedly done aboard a ship on which he was returning to Canada. The *S.S. Dominion* sailed the trans-Atlantic emigration routes from 1870 to 1885.

Better than any worked-up exhibition piece could do, these studies convey a vivid impression of what conditions were like for "huddled masses" on these ships in the nineteenth century.

16. Allan Edson
Emigrant Children, S.S. Dominion.
Pencil, 4¾ x 6⅝ ins (12 x 16.9 cm).
Collection: The Public Archives of Canada, Ottawa.

17. Allan Edson
Morning, Emigrants on Deck.
Pencil, 4¾ x 6½ ins (12 x 16.5 cm).
Collection: The Public Archives of Canada, Ottawa.

Robert Harris
1849–1919

By 1877 Harris was in Paris, where he studied under Léon Bonnat. He was back there in 1881 and, on his return to Canada, was entrusted with the important commission to paint "The Fathers of Confederation," on which he spent two years.

In his entertaining book on the artist, Moncrieff Williamson writes: "Early poverty had taught Harris to concentrate upon what he could do best, and this was to paint portraits." We have good grounds to regret this decision. In some of his genre subjects, such as "Harmony"

in the National Gallery, he displays not only skill but great sensitivity. His less familiar later works, influenced by Impressionism, although discreet in color, are freely and delicately painted.

Pl. 18 is a page from a sketchbook which includes a study for his painting "The News Boy" of 1879, now in the Art Gallery of Ontario. On it Harris has noted that he sent the painting to the O.S.A. exhibition and that "the Marquis of Lorne on seeing this made me A.R.C.A."

18. Robert Harris
Sketchbook Study for "The News Boy", 1879.
Pencil, 3⁹/₁₀ x 6⁷/₁₀ ins (10 x 17 cm). Collection:
The Confederation Art Gallery and Museum,
Charlottetown.

In this drawing Harris has caught the evangelist, Bible in hand, in full voice. It would appear that Moody would have been well qualified to join the ranks of the fraternity of our time. But distance lends enchantment and, on second thought, perhaps we can envision him as a Dickensian character, unlikely to be a social menace like so many of his ilk today. Besides, with his associate Sankey, he did leave us a considerable collection of popular gospel hymns.

19. Robert Harris
The Evangelist Moody, 1887. Pencil and ink, 6¼ x 4 ins (15.9 x 10.2 cm). Collection: The Confederation Art Gallery and Museum, Charlottetown.

R.C.A.–Some Early Members

William Armstrong
1822–1914

Because of the intense interest in the expanding western frontier, many artists made their way to the great plains and the Rockies before the region was opened up by the railways. Among them were Kane, Hind, Armstrong and Verner.

Armstrong came to Canada in 1851 and worked for the railways before he became a full-time painter in the 1880s. He was made an A.R.C.A. in 1882.

Although our drawing is a very early example of his recording of Indian life, it will serve as typical of the subjects which became so familiar in the last decades of the century. Armstrong was one of the most factual reporters (he was also a photographer), but he used his earlier drawings and watercolors as a source for later versions until after the turn of the century.

20. William Armstrong
Watercolor over pencil on prepared ground, 6¾ x 8¹³⁄₁₆ ins (17.1 x 22.3 cm). Collection: The Royal Ontario Museum. Gift of the Imperial Order of the Daughters of the Empire, C. W. Jefferys Chapter, Toronto.

J. W. L. Forster
1850–1938

Forster studied in Paris in 1879, and became an
A.R.C.A. in 1884. A portrait painter, his clients
included many leading Canadians.

The lady in this page of studies is wearing a
tea gown of about 1890—just the thing to slip
into to receive guests! The exercise seems not to
decide on a pose, but to choose from a variety of
facial expressions for the finished work.

21. **J. W. L. Forster**
Studies for a Portrait, c.1890.
Pencil, 10¼ x 8 ins (26 x 20.3 cm).
Collection: The Agnes Ethering-
ton Art Centre, Queen's
University, Kingston.

Edmond Dyonnet
1859–1954

Dyonnet was born in France and studied in Italy. He came to Canada in 1875 and settled in Montreal where he became an art teacher. It comes as a surprise to learn that Jack Bush studied under him. An A.R.C.A. in 1893, he became Secretary to the Academy (1910–47). He specialized in portraiture. All one can claim for such a drawing is that it shows a relentless search for the character of the sitter. Dorothy Stevens later achieved the same result with greater skill. (See Pl. 150.)

22. Edmond Dyonnet
Profile Portrait. Black chalk, 13 x 10½ ins (33 x 26.7 cm).
Collection: The Art Gallery of Ontario.

Frederick S. Challener
1869–1959

Challener settled in Toronto in 1883 where he studied at the Ontario School of Art, and later with G. A. Reid (see Pl. 43).

He is best known for his mural paintings in many parts of Canada. Our drawing may have been a study for a mural. With its classical treatment of draperies, it is a typical example of the discreet nude acceptable at the time.

23. Frederick S. Challener
Nude, 1910. Pencil and chalk, 9³⁄₁₆ x 6³⁄₁₆ ins (23.3 x 15.7 cm). Collection: The Art Gallery of Ontario.

Charles Macdonald Manly
1855–1924

This extremely detailed drawing with its extensive notations relating to tone and color is an example of the most highly developed type of working drawing. The artist has even specified the character of the painting he intended to create from it: "subject was the very rich grass of watercourse and its line-feeling."

Manly taught at the Ontario School of Art, and the younger members of the N.D.S.L. group (see following pages) may have been his students. One of them, F. H. Brigden, died while sketching at Bolton, where this drawing was made.

24. Charles Macdonald Manly
Bolton, 1888. *Dry Bed of Hillside Stream*, Bolton.
Pencil, 6⅙ x 7⅗ ins (15.7 x 19.4 cm). Collection:
The Ontario College of Art.

Nulla Dies Sine Linea Club

In the summer of 1970 John R. Taylor, a staff member of the Ontario College of Art, discovered a large number of drawings by a group of artists active at the turn of the century.

This find at the College brought to light the existence of an unofficial society of artists who had adopted the motto "Nulla Dies Sine Linea," roughly, "No day without a drawing."

Apparently its members, who gained a living by working in print shops and engraving houses, banded together to encourage each other to produce an original drawing in their leisure time every day. Many of the drawings found are inscribed "N.D.S.L.," and some are dedicated to fellow members. Judging by those which are dated, the club was operative between the years 1891 and 1907.

Although it was by no means uncommon for artists to be obliged to earn a living by commercial work (at Notman's Photographic studios in Montreal and Toronto, for example, or Grip Printing & Publishing Co. which later employed members of the Group of Seven), it is nevertheless touching to learn of a group so anxious to assert their dignity as artists as to take such a determined and practical step.

The four following drawings are by members of the club.

Archibald A. Martin
1876–1954

Martin was a nephew of T. Mower Martin (see Pl. 14). As a young man he worked as a commercial artist by day and attended classes at the Ontario School of Art by night.

In 1902 he worked his way to England on a cattle boat and joined a highly successful commercial enterprise in London, the Carlton Studio, of which he became president.

Less labored than the Manly (Pl. 24), Martin's swift pencil has concentrated on tonal contrasts and reads somewhat in the manner of a musical score.

25. **Archibald A. Martin**
Buildings on a Hillside, 1890s. Pencil, 7⅘ x 9⁹⁄₁₀ ins (19.9 x 25.2 cm). Collection: The Ontario College of Art.

Frederick Henry Brigden
1871–1956

Brigden's father was the founder of the well known firm of engravers. It is not surprising, therefore, that he has used his pen here as if it were an engraving tool.

This youthful work (Pl. 26), done while he was a member of the N.D.S.L. group, is inscribed to M. E. Wrinch, who later became the second wife of George Reid (see Pl. 43). Mary Wrinch was about the same age as Brigden and both attended the Ontario School of Art. We may therefore assume that she was also a member of N.D.S.L. Another member was Robert Holmes (1861–1930), painter of botanical subjects.

Brigden's drawing of a woman sewing (Pl. 27) also employs the linear technique of the engraver.

26. Frederick Henry Brigden
Farm, c.1891. Ink over pencil, 7 x 7⁹⁄₁₀ ins (17.9 x 20.3 cm). Inscribed to M. E. Wrinch. Collection: The Ontario College of Art.

F.H.Brigden 1891
To. C. M. Manly.

27. Frederick Henry Brigden
Woman Sewing, 1891. Ink, 8¾ x 6⅔ ins (22.2 x
17 cm). Inscribed to C. M. Manly. Collection:
The Ontario College of Art.

The Barbizon Influence

The Barbizon School, a designation given to a group of French artists, took its name from a village in the Forest of Fontainebleau where they visited to paint the surrounding countryside. Sometimes known as "The Men of Thirty," from the 1830s they brought a fresh approach to landscape painting, and by mid-century had become extremely influential. Anti-classical in their approach, they formed a link between the Romantic movement and the French Impressionists.

Among them, Jean-François Millet, one of the great draughtsmen of the nineteenth century, started a vogue for peasant subjects which spread throughout North America. The result was a flood of paintings representing farm workers viewed in a somewhat sentimental light.

Wyatt Eaton
1849–1896

Eaton, after study in Paris under Gérôme, met Jean-François Millet about 1873/74.

Our drawing is a study for a painting, and bears obvious reference to Millet's subjects, such as "The Sower," "The Angelus" or "The Gleaners."

28. Wyatt Eaton
The Harvest Field. Pencil on gray paper, 8¾ x 8¼ ins (22.2 x 20.9 cm). Collection: The Montreal Museum of Fine Arts. Gift of R. G. Matthews, 1951.

Homer Watson
1855–1936

Here again we have a subject of rural life. It is inscribed: "Homer went to school here while the old stone school house at Strasburgh was torn down and rebuilt in brick." Watson first worked in the Notman studio in Toronto and then visited the United States in 1876, where he came under the influence of the Hudson River School. Between 1887 and 1890 he was in England.

Although his name has frequently been associated with Constable (probably due to Oscar Wilde naming him "The Canadian Constable"), his work of the 1890s is closer to that of the Barbizon School, whose paintings were then in great demand in North America.

Despite the fact that he received much acclaim and considerable financial success at the height of his career, Watson outlived his time and died a bankrupt in Doon, where he had spent most of his life.

29. Homer Watson
Sketchbook 2, page 62a. Graphite, ink and wash,
17¼ x 14 ins (43.8 x 35.6 cm). Collection: The
National Gallery of Canada.

Horatio Walker
1858–1938

Walker prospered by maintaining a close connection with the United States throughout his professional career.

He is best known for his paintings of the Île d'Orléans where he settled in 1883. Before that he visited Europe and came under the influence of the Barbizon School. This can be detected in this powerful drawing which reflects the current interest in and respect for labor on the land.

30. Horatio Walker
Labour (or Oxen). Charcoal, 17 x 23 ins (43.2 x 59 cm). Collection: The Agnes Etherington Art Centre, Queen's University, Kingston.

Georges Chavignaud
1865–1944

I have reproduced both sides of this drawing to show the two beautiful studies of peasant women, and to call attention to the fact that artists often used both sides of a sheet of paper— or a sketch panel for that matter.

The small vignette on the reverse looks very much like a Homer Watson Doon landscape. As for the heads, their expressive quality could not be improved by any elaboration in the oil medium.

31. Georges Chavignaud
Recto: *Study of a Peasant Woman*. Black chalk, 8 x 6½ ins (20.3 x 16.5 cm).

32. Verso: *Page of Studies*. Black chalk, 9 x 7¼ ins (22.9 x 18.4 cm). Private collection, Toronto.

Marc-Aurèle de Foy Suzor-Coté
1869–1937

Suzor-Coté first visited Paris in 1890. After study he exhibited regularly at the Salon.

A measure of how far Canadian art had fallen behind the European experience may be found in this fine drawing (Pl. 33), exhibited at the British Empire Exhibition in 1924. Obviously it is influenced by Jean-François Millet, but the artist's concern may not have been so much with the peasant as with current modes of the Canadian market. About the peasant studies of Van Gogh (also based on the work of Millet) we have no such doubts, but by 1924 Van Gogh had been dead for more than thirty years. The engaging study of a young Edwardian lady (Pl. 34) was probably closer to Suzor-Coté's real sentimental interests.

33. **Marc-Aurèle de Foy Suzor-Coté**
Peasant Working in a Field, c.1924. Charcoal, 11 x 10 ins (27.9 x 25.4 cm). Miss Warda Drummond, Montreal.

34. **Suzor-Coté**
Portrait of a Young Lady. Black and white chalk on brown paper, 6 ¾ x 4 ½ ins (17.1 x 11.4 cm). Private collection.

Popular Art: The Illustrators

Charles Macdonald Manly
1855–1924

Manly (see Pl. 24) was associated with the Toronto Art Students League, founded in 1886, which included Brigden (see Pl. 26) and Jefferys (see Pl. 37). From 1892 to 1904 the League published an illustrated calendar. Membership consisted of artists engaged in commercial work who met for study and sketching trips.

35. **Charles Macdonald Manly**
Champlain Market, Quebec, from Point Levis. Ink, 13⅘ x 9 ins (35.1 x 23 cm). Collection: The Ontario College of Art.

Henri Julien
1852–1908

Julien worked as a cartoonist and illustrator for Montreal newspapers and periodicals. He was particularly interested in customs of the habitants.

In 1874 he accompanied the expedition of the North West Mounted Police to suppress liquor traffic on the prairies, and contributed scenes of Western life to the *Canadian Illustrated News*.

36. Henri Julien
Country Dance. Ink, 15¾ x 11 ins (40 x 28.4 cm). Collection: The McCord Museum, Montreal.

Charles William Jefferys
1869–1952

Jefferys settled in Toronto in 1880, where he worked for newspapers.

Subsequently he became an illustrator for the *New York Herald* in 1892, and returned to Toronto in 1899.

He is best known for his illustrations in *Chronicles of Canada* and as author of *The*

Picture Gallery of Canadian History. Our drawing is the original for an illustration in his *Canada's Past in Pictures*, published by Ryerson Press.

37. C. W. Jefferys
The Brothers Vérendrye in sight of the Western Mountains. Ink, 13⅜ x 17½ ins (34 x 44.5 cm).
Private collection.

Edmond Joseph Massicote
1875–1929

Massicote studied under Dyonnet (see Pl. 22) in Montreal, then worked as a freelance illustrator for various French Canadian publications. He specialized in customs, costumes and details of early Canadian life.

Our drawing appears to be connected with the illustrations to his publication *Nos Canadiens d'Autrefois*, Granger Frères, 1923.

38. Edmond Joseph Massicote
Un magasin général de jadis, 1925. Ink with wash, 19¹⁄₁₆ x 24¾ ins (49.8 x 62.9 cm). Collection: Musée du Québec.

The Lure of Paris

In the last decades of the nineteenth century Canadians flocked to Europe to complete their training, most of them attending the École des Beaux-Arts, or schools such as Julian's or Colarossi's. Among their teachers were the renowned academicians Cabanel, Gérôme, Carolus-Duran, Boulanger and Bouguereau.

The academies everywhere insisted on "correct" drawing; in fact students were not encouraged to proceed to painting classes until they had satisfied that requirement by study, first from plaster casts, and later in the life class. The Male Nude (Pl. 39) is an example of Gagnon's student work in Montreal.

As a result of this process even the least talented were able to produce a respectable drawing. I am not suggesting that such training has no value: even the greatest talent can only achieve its potential through devoted application. As Tintoretto wrote: ". . . good drawings can only be fetched from the casket of the artist's talent with patient study and sleepless nights."

What most Canadians brought back from Paris was competence to produce the typical "Salon" painting. Every one of the eight artists included in this section studied there.

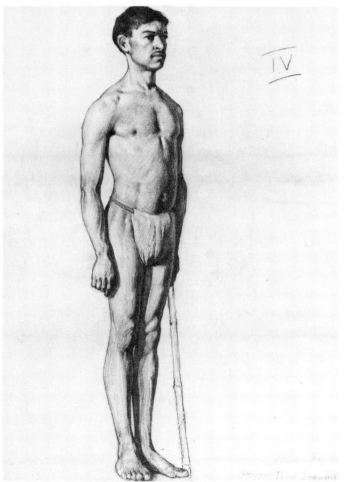

39. Clarence Gagnon
Male Nude, 1900–01. Charcoal, 24 x 17 ins (61 x 43.2 cm). Inscribed: Time Drawing. Collection: The Montreal Museum of Fine Arts.

William Brymner
1855–1925

Brymner was the first to arrive in Paris in 1876, and he remained there for nine years. On his return he became a teacher at the Art Association of Montreal, and many of Canada's best artists began their careers under his instruction.

Our drawing may have been a study for one of the domestic scenes in which he specialized. This masterly work provides an excellent example of the difference between schooled facility and inborn talent. The element required to raise a drawing above competence is vision—the capacity to express perception in plastic terms (call it "plastic intelligence" if you will). With extreme economy Brymner succeeds in capturing both the psychological and physical aspects of the subject, and one can almost reconstruct the decisive movements of his pencil.

40. William Brymner
Page from a Sketchbook, c.1885. Graphite, 4⅙ x 3½ ins (10.6 x 9.3 cm). Collection: The Art Gallery of Hamilton. Gift of R. W. Pilot, R.C.A.

Charles Huot
1855–1930

Huot was a Quebec muralist who depended on church commissions for a large part of his living.

Our drawing is reminiscent of similar works by Lhermitte, one of the later Barbizon painters who worked in the spirit of Millet.

41. Charles Huot
Chapelle de l'Hôpital Général à Québec. Charcoal, 20 x 12⅜ ins (50.8 x 31.4 cm).
Collection: Musée du Québec.

F. McGillivray Knowles
1859–1932

Like Huot in Montreal, Knowles in Toronto found mural painting lucrative: in his case for the most part in private homes.

In this drawing he is trying out two alternative compositions for a mural depicting some ritualistic or ceremonial occasion. It is hardly surprising that few working drawings of this description have survived as they were intended solely for the artist's use.

42. **F. McG. Knowles**
Study for Mural (Ardnold).
Pencil, 15 x 11⅛ ins (45.7 x 28.3 cm). Collection: The Art Gallery of Ontario. Gift of the Gordon Conn–F. S. McGillivray Knowles Trust, 1969.

George Agnew Reid
1860–1947

This charming portrait drawing in charcoal was obviously intended to be a finished work rather than a study for an oil painting.

Such portraits on paper take their place between miniatures and canvases. Proceeding from a long tradition, they were particularly favored in the eighteenth century.

Reid was an academician par excellence. He became President of the R.C.A. in 1906 and was Principal of the Ontario College of Art from 1912 to 1928. His studio in Toronto was furnished with all the attributes of a recognized *maître*.

43. George Agnew Reid
Hattie, 1880. Charcoal, 13½ x 9 ins (34.3 x 22.9 cm). Collection: The London Regional Art Gallery. Gift of Mrs. G. A. Reid.

Paul Peel
1860–1891

This drawing (Pl. 44) was probably made while Peel was a student at the R.A. Schools, London, in 1880.

It is interesting in the light of the fact that before the famous English painters George Frederick Watts and Frederic Leighton had brought about a renewed interest in Roman and Grecian subjects in the 1860s, the Elgin marbles had been regarded merely as curiosities. Thereafter they attracted the attention of many artists, such as Albert Moore. It would therefore be natural for Peel, as a student, to visit the British Museum to study them.

I have always thought that Peel was one of the most gifted of Canadian artists. At the age of seventeen he was already studying at the Pennsylvania Academy. He went on to continue his studies in London and Paris.

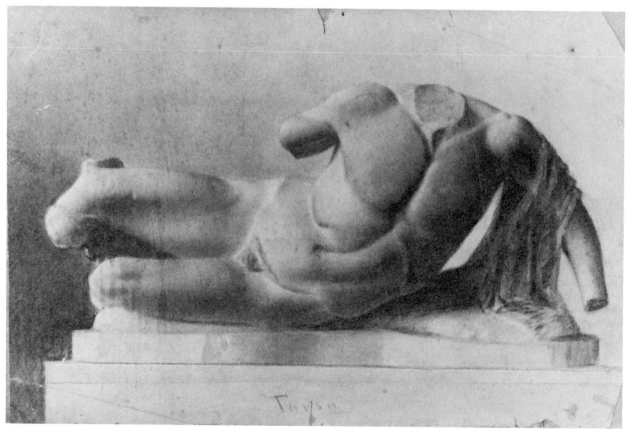

44. Paul Peel
Torso: Study from the Elgin Marbles. Pencil, 10¾ x 16 ins (27.3 x 40.6 cm). Collection: The London Regional Art Gallery. Gift of Mr. J. A. Tillman, London.

45. Paul Peel (opposite)
Portrait of the Artist's Wife, 1885. Graphite, 10 x 7½ ins (25.4 x 19.1 cm). Collection: The National Gallery of Canada.

His development was cut short by his early
death at the age of thirty-one. At that time he
was still an academic painter, but we may at
least claim for him that his work was on a par
with that of his master Gérôme.

Sidney Strickland Tully
1860–1911

Tully was one of a number of women who were able to pursue the career of professional artists in the second half of the nineteenth century. Previous to that time it was difficult, if not impossible. She studied at the Ontario School of Art, the Slade in London and at the Julian and Colarossi academies in Paris.

This drawing is a study for the painting "Twilight of Life" in the collection of the Art Gallery of Ontario, which was a Gold Medal winner at the Pan-American Exposition of 1908. The sense of resignation to a sedentary existence, the lateness of the hour symbolized by the clock, and the title convey the sentimentality of the period.

46. Sidney Strickland Tully
Twilight of Life. Ink, 7⅔ x 6⅙ ins (19.4 x 15.7 cm). Collection: The Ontario College of Art.

James Macdonald Barnsley
1861–1929

Like the Brymner (Pl. 40) this drawing is a
virtuoso performance. The tonal control is so
precise that one is almost persuaded of the
validity of the claim made by some writers on art
that an artist can suggest color while restricting
himself to the use of black and white.

47. James Macdonald Barnsley
Sketch book: Construction Site. Pencil, 6⅛ x
3⅝ ins (15.3 x 9.2 cm). Collection: The Montreal
Museum of Fine Art. Gift of Robert P. Jellett.

Georges Delfosse
1869–1939

Delfosse studied under Brymner (see Pl. 40) and later in Paris. He painted pictures for St. James's Cathedral in Montreal.

With the arch indicated at the top, this drawing appears to be a study for a large painting or altarpiece.

In style it is neither Baroque nor Neo-Classical: there is about it a peculiarly Victorian air. It reminds one somewhat of the drawings of Frederic Leighton. Perhaps the fervor in religious painting was beginning to cool by Delfosse's time.

48. Georges Delfosse
The Deposition. Black chalk with pastel on brown paper, 15¼ x 21 ins (38.7 x 53.3 cm). Collection: The Kaspar Gallery, Toronto.

R.C.A.–Continued

Like most self-perpetuating societies, the Academies of England and Canada have outlived their function, both as exhibiting bodies and as representatives of a majority of the most creative contemporary artists.

That is not to say that the R.C.A. has not been able at any one time (including the present) to enlist a number of distinguished artists. After all, membership still carries with it a certain prestige, and to refuse the honor implied requires a strong conviction on the part of the artist that it cannot be accepted without compromising standards.

So, before closing the book on the Academy, I have included here three drawings by members, all of whom were born at the turn of the century.

Robert Pilot
1898–1967

Born in Newfoundland, Pilot moved to Montreal in 1911. He studied with Cullen (see Pl. 56) and Brymner (see Pl. 40). In 1952 he became President of the R.C.A.

49. Robert Pilot
Chambly, 1925. Pencil and sepia ink, 5¼ x 10¼ ins (13.3 x 26 cm). Collection: Mr. and Mrs. Fred Schaeffer.

John Alfsen
1902–1971

Alfsen was born in Michigan and moved to Toronto in 1915. He studied at the Ontario College of Art (where he later became a teacher) and at the Art Students League in New York.

Although there is a certain tentativeness about this drawing, it does demonstrate the kind of competence maintained by Academy standards.

50. John Alfsen
Woman Sleeping, 1930. Red conté, 12¼ x 19 ins (31.1 x 48.3 cm). Collection: The National Gallery of Canada.

Herbert S. Palmer
1881–1970

Palmer studied at the Central Ontario School of Art under Challener (Pl. 51).

Elected A.R.C.A. in 1915, he painted for the Canadian War Memorials in the First World War. He became a full academician in 1934 and served as Secretary to the Academy from 1948 to 1951.

Palmer painted landscapes and animals, particularly sheep—in fact one might call him the Canadian Jacque (a Barbizon painter).

This is a page of studies, probably of the child of his teacher Challener.

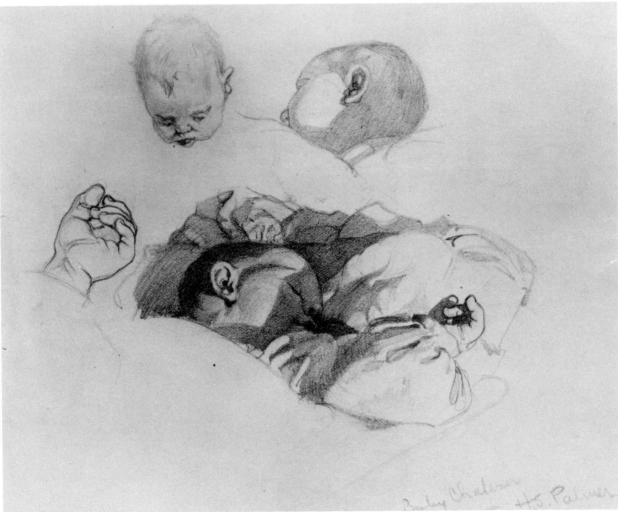

51. Herbert S. Palmer
Baby Challener, 1908. Pencil, 7⅛ x 8½ ins (18.1 x 21.6 cm). Signed, inscribed and dated. Collection: The Art Gallery of Ontario. Canada Council Joint Purchase Fund, 1961.

A Quebec Visionary

Ozias Leduc
1864–1955

Leduc subsisted almost entirely on his work as a church decorator. It was in this capacity that Borduas (see Pls. 103, 104) was apprenticed to him.

Our drawing (Pl. 52) is a design on the theme of "The Last Supper," squared for enlargement as a church mural or altarpiece.

He was born in the small town of Saint-Hilaire and spent his whole life there, making only one brief visit abroad in 1897 to Paris with Suzor-Coté (see Pls. 33, 34).

Apart from his work for the church, Leduc's oeuvre was small. He pursued his private vision which, at first reminiscent of eighteenth century masters such as Chardin and Greuze, brought him in his last years to symbolism. His relative seclusion and total integrity eventually attracted the attention of a group of devoted admirers.

52. Ozias Leduc
Study for The Last Supper. Ink with pastel, 5½ x 7 ins (14 x 17.8 cm). Squared for enlargement. Private collection, Toronto.

This drawing (Pl. 53) is remarkably close to the finished painting in the National Gallery, on which Leduc spent seven years. The only significant difference is that the bowl, out of scale in the drawing, was reduced in the painting and a crust of bread added on the table.

The painting, now titled "L'Enfant au pain," has also been known as "Le musicien," suggesting that the addition of the bread had considerable symbolic significance for the artist.

53. Ozias Leduc
Study for "L'Enfant au pain," 1896. Charcoal, 18¾ x 21⅜ ins (47.6 x 54.3 cm). Collection: The National Gallery of Canada.

Morrice and Canadian Impressionism

The radicalism of the French Impressionists who first exhibited in 1874 consisted in their scientific study of light and color, which led them to apply paint in small strokes of pure unmixed color to give the effect of light striking on surfaces.

The universal effect of their discoveries on their followers in North America was to cause them to lighten their palettes without abandoning their primarily naturalistic intentions. In other words, Impressionism was widely adopted in a superficial manner.

Apart from the direct contact with Impressionism in Paris which influenced some Canadians studying there, the most important connection with the movement was established through the expatriate artist James Wilson Morrice.

Morrice returned to Canada frequently until the First World War, and painted around the Isle d'Orléans with Brymner (Pl. 40), Cullen (Pl. 56) and Edmund Morris. He also exhibited regularly with the forward-looking Canadian Art Club, formed in 1907.

James Wilson Morrice 1865–1924

Morrice's sojourn in Paris began in 1889 and, except for visits abroad, he remained there for the rest of his life. Because of the close relationship he retained with his native land, and his frequent painting trips there, he has rightly been claimed as one of Canada's greatest masters, but the style he evolved was purely French.

Located as he was at the center of the art world, his contacts were many. Two of them were crucial; first with Whistler and later with Matisse. His mature work can perhaps be described as occupying a position between the Fauves and the Nabis.

His influence on Canadian art was profound, and may be traced to the next generation in the works of Gagnon, Robinson, Lyman and Jackson.

Because Morrice devoted his life to *belle peinture*, we shall not find many drawings. Most of them are pages from his sketchbooks, notations for future paintings. Both the drawings reproduced here fall into that category.

54. **James Wilson Morrice** (above)
Riverside Promenade. Black chalk, 5 x 10 ins (12.7 x 25.4 cm). Collection: Mr. Gerry Moses.

55. **James Wilson Morrice** (below)
Kingston, Jamaica, 1915. Pencil and wash, $9\frac{9}{10}$ x $12\frac{1}{2}$ ins (25.1 x 31.7 cm). The McMichael Canadian Collection, Kleinburg, Ontario.

Maurice Cullen
1866–1934

Cullen went to Paris in 1888 and, after study at the École des Beaux-Arts, remained there to paint and exhibit at the Salon. In 1895 he returned to Montreal, where he became a member of the Canadian Art Club.

He was a close friend of Morrice and painted with him in Brittany, Venice and Beaupré, near Quebec City.

In 1918 he was enlisted to work for the Canadian War Memorials, at which time our drawing was made.

56. **Maurice Cullen**
Camblain l'Abbé, 1919. Pencil, 9¼ x 12¼ ins (23.5 x 31.1 cm). Collection: The Art Gallery of Hamilton. Gift of R. W. Pilot, R.C.A.

Clarence Gagnon
1881–1942

After studying under Brymner (see Pl. 40), Gagnon went to Paris in 1904, where he enrolled at the Julian academy. He became an admirer of Morrice. After his return to Montreal in 1909 he divided his time between Canada and Europe. He is best known for his paintings of rural Quebec and its people.

In his most famous work, the illustrations for *Maria Chapdelaine*, he introduced an element of symbolism to add a more universal significance to the legend.

58. Clarence Gagnon (below)
Village Street, Charlevoix, Quebec. Study for a painting in the Art Gallery of Ontario. Pencil, 8 x 13 ins (20.3 x 33 cm). Private collection.

57. Clarence Gagnon (above)
Boy Warming Hands. Watercolor and pencil, 6⅕ x 7½ ins (15.8 x 19 cm). Collection: The Art Gallery of Greater Victoria.

Albert H. Robinson
1881–1956

After study in Paris, Robinson returned to his home town, Hamilton, where he taught at the Art School. About 1908 he moved to Montreal.

Of all Canadian artists Robinson came closest in adapting Morrice's aesthetic to the Quebec scene.

In 1910 he met A. Y. Jackson and painted with him in Brittany. His continuing friendship with Jackson firmed the link between Morrice and the Group of Seven.

Pl. 60 is a rare figure study which also reveals a debt to his master.

59. Albert H. Robinson
Quebec Farm. Pencil, 7 x 8 ins (17.8 x 20.3 cm).
Collection: The Tom Thomson Memorial
Gallery, Owen Sound.

60. Albert H. Robinson
Nude, 1906. Pencil, 12 x 9¼ ins (30.5 x 23.5 cm).
Collection: The McMichael Canadian Collection,
Kleinburg, Ontario.

Frederick S. Coburn
1871–1960

After extensive study in Europe, Coburn returned to Canada in 1898. He specialized in winter landscapes, and painted innumerable pictures of logging teams in a watered-down Impressionist style.

    This fresh little drawing shows him at his liveliest.

61. Frederick S. Coburn
The Red Sleigh. Pastel, 8 ½ x 10 ¼ ins (21.6 x 26 cm). Collection: Mr. & Mrs. Fred Schaeffer.

Herbert Raine
1875–1951

Trained in the R. A. Schools, London, Raine came to Montreal early in the century. He practiced as an architect, and developed a special interest in etchings and watercolor scenes of old Montreal and rural Quebec.

He became a member of the Pen and Pencil Club, Montreal, in 1916, which is probably about the time when this drawing was made.

I have included it in this section because of its Impressionist style.

62. Herbert Raine
Habitant Woman peeling Potatoes, Beaupré.
Pencil, 9⁵/₁₆ x 7⅛ ins (23.7 x 18 cm). Collection:
Musée du Québec.

Group of Seven

Tom Thomson
1877–1917

The intention of the Group of Seven, formed in 1920, was to create a national school of landscape painting. The style they adopted turned out to be the combination of a restrained use of Fauve color with a swirling Art Nouveau line.

Because their aim in depicting the Canadian scene was in the main painterly, most of their drawings which have survived are working plans for paintings: indeed one suspects that they were made only when circumstances prevented the painting of oil sketches on the spot.

Although Thomson did not live long enough to become a formal member of the Group of Seven, his work can only be considered in that context. Like most of the members of the Group, he began his career by working as a commercial artist for the firm of Grip in Toronto.

This early page from a sketchbook bears the stamp of the commercial illustrator.

63. Tom Thomson
Two Ladies and a Girl. Pencil, 8¾ x 5¼ ins
(22.2 x 13.3 cm). Collection: The Tom Thomson
Memorial Gallery, Owen Sound.

J. E. H. MacDonald
1873–1932

As is the case with many drawings of the Group, this MacDonald reflects his experience as a commercial artist.

Along with many other artists of the period, they sought to amplify their income by producing prints of various kinds, including silk-screens.

For a short time in 1904 MacDonald worked for the Carlton Studio in London, England, where Archibald Martin had preceded him (see Pl. 25).

64. J. E. H. MacDonald
Lake in the Rockies. Chalk, ink and gouache,
11¼ x 9½ ins (28.6 x 24 cm). Private collection.

Lawren Harris
1885–1970

This early drawing appears to be designed for reproduction as a print. It is one of a long series he made depicting working class districts in Toronto, and reflects his European training.

65. Lawren Harris
Toronto Houses, c.1918–21. Ink, 8⅝ x 11 ins
(21.9 x 27.9 cm). Private collection.

A. Y. Jackson
1882–1974

In this drawing the artist simply records the bare
bones of the subject. Although he was only concerned to register his composition for future use,
he does carry it off with a sort of rollicking
verve.

66. A. Y. Jackson
Maynooth, Ontario, c.1935. Pencil, 8½ x 11 ins
(21.6 x 27.9 cm). Private collection.

A. J. Casson
1898–

This is a good example of a drawing intended as a guide for a future painting. Done in the year when Casson became a member of the Group, the color areas are defined with the simplicity of a cartoon, yet all the information the artist needs is there.

67. A. J. Casson
Elora, 1926. Pencil, 8¼ x 10¾ ins (21 x 27.3 cm).
Private collection.

Arthur Lismer
1885–1969

The two members of the original Group of Seven who valued drawing as a medium in its own right and not simply as a preparatory stage in the painting process were Lismer and Varley. Like all fine draughtsmen, they constantly practiced their art, and a large number of their drawings have survived.

Lismer's nervous line tends at times to be overactive, and his compositions cluttered. At their best his drawings have a powerful controlled energy.

In 1933, when this drawing was done (Pl. 68), Emily Carr was still an exciting new personality to members of the Group of Seven. Lismer's keen eye and practiced hand have captured the character we know through *Klee Wyck*.

68. Arthur Lismer
Emily Carr with her Monkey and Dogs, **1933. Pen and black chalk, 7¼ x 9¼ ins (18.4 x 23.5 cm). Collection: The National Gallery of Canada.**

69. Arthur Lismer
Mattawa, **c.1930. Pencil, 10¼ x 13¾ ins (26 x 34.9 cm). Private collection.**

Frederick H. Varley
1881–1969

In talent, sensibility and range, Varley surpassed all other members of the Group.

During the First World War he was an official war artist—the one who was able to convey his feelings most convincingly. He did this in symbolic terms. In the drawing reproduced here (Pl. 71) Varley employs the broken image of Christ, lying on the ground against a background of marching soldiers, to express his horror of the inexorable demand for sacrifice. But he was also able to celebrate his joy at the end of the agony of both world wars in canvases titled "Liberation." The larger, at the Art Gallery of Ontario, is the greatest Canadian religious painting of the century.

As can be seen here (Pl. 70) his landscape drawings fully exploit the resources of the medium.

On the rare occasions when he was persuaded to paint portraits, he always managed to produce a painting of value beyond the historical record, and his drawings of women rival those of Augustus John in beauty (Pl. 72).

70. **Frederick H. Varley** (left)
Reflections in the Lake, c.1935–6. Location is
Rice Lake, B.C. Pencil and watercolor, 11½ x
14¾ ins (29 x 37.5 cm). Private collection.

71. **Frederick H. Varley** (right)
The Christ Tree, 1918. Watercolor over graphite,
6⅞ x 9¹⁵⁄₁₆ ins (17.5 x 25.2 cm). Collection: The
National Gallery of Canada.

72. **Frederick H. Varley** (below)
Head. Charcoal, 8½ x 10 ins (21.6 x 25.4 cm).
Collection: Art Gallery of Greater Victoria. Gift
of Harold Mortimer–Lamb.

Edwin H. Holgate
1892–1977

Holgate, who was invited to join the Group of Seven in 1931, had previously been associated with a number of Montreal artists in what came to be known as the Beaver Hall Group, formed in 1920.

Holgate was always more interested in the figure than in landscape, though he managed to combine the two subjects successfully in a series of paintings.

The monumental nude (Pl. 74) is typical of the figures which he later introduced into his Canadian landscapes.

73. Edwin H. Holgate
Stairway, Natashiquan, c.1934. The subject is the artist's wife in their cottage. Pencil, 11 x 8 ins (27.9 x 20.3 cm). Private collection.

74. Edwin H. Holgate
Nude holding her ankle, c.1938. Colored chalks, 11 x 7¾ ins (27.9 x 19.7 cm). Private collection.

Towards Non-Objective Art

Bertram Brooker
1888–1955

In the late 1920s a favorable climate was developing for the emergence of Non-Objective art in Canada. Lawren Harris and Fred Housser were propagating the doctrines of Theosophy, and Kandinsky's book *Concerning the Spiritual in Art* was becoming widely known. Brooker heard all this discussed at the Arts and Letters Club in Toronto and, while others theorized, he painted. His exhibition of Non-Objective canvases at the Club in 1927 was the first of its kind.

The subsequent Non-Objective paintings of Brooker (Pl. 75), Harris (Pl. 77) and Fitz-Gerald (Pl. 79) were based on a search for transcendent spiritual values felt to be inherent in all natural phenomena (the Theosophical credo) and had nothing to do with later developments in Montreal, which had their source in Surrealism.

The drawing (Pl. 76) was done after his meeting with FitzGerald, under whose influence Brooker turned away from Non-Objective art.

75. Bertram Brooker
Interiors within Interiors (Whitman), 1931. Ink, 8 x 11 ins (20.3 x 27.9 cm). Collection: The Brooker Estate.

76. Bertram Brooker
Study of Trees. Pencil, 8¾ x 11½ ins (22.2 x 29 cm). Private collection.

Lawren Harris
1885–1970

Although Harris towards the end of his life reached for total Non-Objectivity, most of his late works are abstracted from nature. We can find here (Pl. 77) symbols for mountains, sun and water. His final resolutions sought to represent forces which Theosophists believe to invest the universe. The mystic powers he tried to evoke do not emerge. The results border on the naive. In order to achieve potency, signs in painting must partake of the quality of icons.

77. Lawren Harris
Abstract Drawing. Pencil, 8½ x 10⅞ ins (21.6 x 27.5 cm). Collection: The Loranger Gallery, Toronto.

78. Lionel LeMoine FitzGerald
Apples, 1954. Colored pencil, 17½ x 37⅞ ins
(44.5 x 96.2 cm). Collection: The National
Gallery of Canada.

79. Lionel LeMoine FitzGerald
Long Abstract, 1955. Pen and colored chalk, 8 x
18¼ ins (20.3 x 46.4 cm). Collection: The
National Gallery of Canada.

Lionel LeMoine FitzGerald
1890–1956

Brooker met FitzGerald in 1929 in Winnipeg, the
beginning of a fruitful relationship maintained
by regular correspondence. Initially Brooker was
strongly influenced by FitzGerald while, towards
the end of his life, the latter produced some Non-
Objective works, probably at the instance of his
friend.

FitzGerald, who lived in Winnipeg, became
a member of the Group of Seven in 1932. His
constant pre-occupation was to define forms in
space. Although he is sometimes referred to as a
Pointillist because of his use of small facets of
paint to build up his structure, the real source of
his refined art is to be found in Cézanne.
Whether the subject be still life, nudes, or landscape, he was concerned to set form against
form, edge against edge, in an orchestrated
design in space.

A comparison of these two drawings (Pls.
78, 79) yields convincing evidence of the path to
abstraction adopted by the Brooker-Harris-
FitzGerald group. The starting point was always
to be found in the perceptible world.

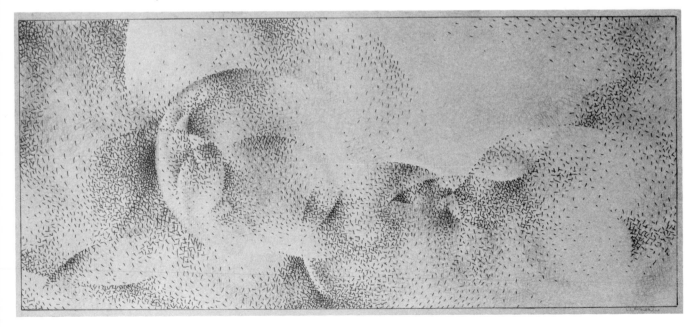

The Contemporary Art Society

John Lyman
1886–1967

The return to Canada of John Lyman in 1931 after about eighteen years in France brought to attention the more formal aspects of Morrice's work. Lyman had also studied under Matisse. In 1939 he founded the Contemporary Art Society in Montreal, which sought by means of exhibitions to introduce the work of contemporary European artists, and to encourage in its members an interest in "the formal qualities of art and a broader subjective response."

Pl. 81 is an example of the new approach to drawing in which the vitality of the line takes precedence over the definition of the model. It reminds us of the drawings Rodin made before moving models. There is also an aura of Art Nouveau or Jugendstil about it which recalls the drawings of Gustav Klimt. But, above all, there is here an echo of Matisse's statement: "As soon as my line—inspired, so to speak, with a life of its own—has molded the light of the empty sheet . . . I stop, I can no longer add or change. The page is written, no correction is possible."

The West Indian drawing (Pl. 80) may be compared with the Morrice (Pl. 55).

80. **John Lyman** (above)
Beach in the West Indies. Crayon and watercolor, 8½ x 12¾ ins (21.6 x 32.4 cm). Collection: Manuge Galleries Ltd., Halifax.

81. **John Lyman**
Dancing Nude. Pencil, 12 x 9 ins (30.5 x 22.9 cm). Collection: Mr. Chris Yaneff, Toronto.

Goodridge Roberts
1904–1974

In 1932 Lyman gave Goodridge Roberts his first critical recognition.

Roberts said that the first good exhibition he saw was the Morrice Retrospective in 1925, while he was still a student at the Beaux-Arts in Montreal. He joined the Contemporary Art Society as a charter member in 1939.

He subsequently became one of Canada's greatest landscape painters, bringing to his work an absolutely uncompromising integrity.

His figure paintings, at first influenced by Matisse, became more expressionistic in his later years.

82. Goodridge Roberts
Gatineau Landscape. Brush, 16¾ x 20¾ ins (29.7 x 52.7 cm). Collection: The National Gallery of Canada.

83. Goodridge Roberts
Standing Nude. Charcoal, 28⅞ x 18 ins (73.3 x 45.3 cm). Collection: Mrs. Joan Roberts.

Stanley Cosgrove
1911–

A pupil of Holgate and early admirer of Good-ridge Roberts, Cosgrove has retained a classic approach to the nude.

If a similarity is detectable between Cosgrove's work and that of Derain, who participated in the classical revival in France after the First World War, it might be explained by the likelihood that he would have seen the latter's canvases in exhibitions organized by the Contemporary Art Society.

This work in oil is a useful reminder that the definition of a drawing depends on its linear quality and has nothing to do with the medium used.

84. Stanley Cosgrove
Study for a Painting, 1950. Oil on paper, 35⅜ x 24¼ ins (89.9 x 61.6 cm). Collection: The Art Gallery of Ontario. Gift from the Albert H. Robson Memorial Subscription Fund, 1951.

Jacques de Tonnancour
1917–

De Tonnancour studied under Goodridge Roberts. In this early drawing the influence of Matisse is particularly evident.

In 1946 he exhibited with the Contemporary Art Society at the Art Association of Montreal.

Like Roberts, his subjects included still life, figure and landscape. Subsequently he became a Non-Objective painter.

85.
Jacques de Tonnancour
Femme assise, 1944.
Pen and black ink,
$23^{15}/_{16}$ x $17^{15}/_{16}$ ins
(60.8 x 45.5 cm).
Collection: The National
Gallery of Canada.

The City and Its People

Philip Surrey
1910–

Surrey was one of the first Canadians to study at the Art Students League in New York instead of in Paris.

The upsurge of interest in regional subject matter and social realism in the United States, spurred by the Depression and the W.P.A. projects, found its counterpart in Canada in renewed interest in subjects related to the urban scene rather than landscape.

Surrey, a friend of Lyman, exhibited with the Contemporary Art Society. His constant preoccupation has been to paint the Montreal scene and the life of the city streets.

86. Philip Surrey
Three Girls, 1970. Charcoal and wash, 16 x 24 ins (40.6 x 61 cm). Private collection.

Lillian Freiman
1908–

Freiman also attended the Art Students League, and later returned to remain in New York.

This pensive early self-portrait may depict the artist bundled up against the cold of her studio, but it may be that she envisioned herself in Renaissance guise—indeed, the drawing reminds one somewhat of Cranach's figures.

87. Lillian Freiman
Early Self-Portrait. Pastel and graphite, 10⁷/₁₆ x 10¼ ins (26.5 x 26.4 cm). Collection: The National Gallery of Canada.

Louis Muhlstock
1904–

Muhlstock returned from his studies in Paris at a time when the effects of the Depression were beginning to be felt in Canada.

A proclaimed socialist, he contributed to several left-wing publications. His drawings of the sick and the poor are moving testaments to his compassionate nature.

88. Louis Muhlstock
Paranka. Charcoal, 15⅝ x 11⅝ ins (39.7 x 29.5 cm). Collection: The National Gallery of Canada.

Marian Scott
1906–

Scott was a founding member of the Contemporary Art Society. By that time she also had turned her attention to urban scenes, particularly as they related to the workers.

This drawing, employing a strong expressionist style, echoes the sentiment of the Muhlstock head (Pl. 88).

89. Marian Scott
Head, c.1947. Oil on paper, 14½ x 11½ ins (36.7 x 29 cm). Collection: the artist.

Fritz Brandtner
1896–1969

Brandtner emigrated to Canada from Danzig in 1928. He was the first European to reach Canada with full knowledge of all the latest developments in art, and found, to his surprise, little awareness of them.

He is best known for his links with German Expressionism. This aspect of his work is represented by the brilliant little ink drawing "Gaspé" (Pl. 90). But he was also one of the pioneers of Non-Objective art in Canada. His work in this field differed from the Transcendentalists, and

was rather a projection of Bauhaus principles. As he himself put it: "The division of the surface spaces is for me the sole object of painting, dreams in the abstract also."

Brandtner was a socialist, and in 1936 held an exhibition in Montreal under the sponsorship of The League Against War and Fascism.

His interest in the working man is evident in the paintings he made in 1942 related to industry in wartime. Our drawing (Pl. 91) is one of this series.

90. Fritz Brandtner
Gaspé, 1950. Colored inks, 5½ x 8 ins (14 x 20.3 cm). Private collection.

91. Fritz Brandtner
Drilling Holes in Plates, Canadian Vickers, 1942. Black and colored inks, 18 x 23⅘ ins (45.6 x 60.5 cm). McMaster University Collection, Hamilton.

Miller Brittain
1912–1968

Brittain was another student at the Art Students League, and the direction of his interest in subject matter is allied to that of the Ash Can School in New York.

This crude but powerful drawing (Pl. 92) is evidence of his concern with the social problems of the 1930s. During the war he served in the R.C.A.F. After this experience he was unable to come to terms with the aftermath; he became something of a recluse and his art turned to fantasy.

The "Female Head" (Pl. 93) shows his raw sensitivity to pain in others.

92. Miller Brittain (above)
Workers Arise, 1936. Carbon pencil, 25 x 19 ins (63.5 x 48.3 cm). Collection: Mr. John Saywell, Toronto.

93. Miller Brittain
Female Head, c.1947. Brown chalk, 10 x 7 ins (25.4 x 17.8 cm). Collection: Galerie Dresdnere, Toronto.

Pegi Nicol MacLeod
1904–1949

Pegi Nicol contributed drawings to *The Canadian Forum*, an organ of the C.C.F. She lived in Toronto from 1934 to 1937, after which she married and moved to New York. Throughout her life she was a devoted observer of the human scene, mostly in cityscapes.

94. Pegi Nicol MacLeod
Amateur Hockey, c.1934. Wash drawing, 24½ x 19½ ins (62 x 49.5 cm). Collection: Esso Resources Canada Ltd.

Paraskeva Clark
1898–

Paraskeva Clark is another artist with a strong social conscience, calling for the participation of artists in the struggle for freedom and justice in the 1930s. Apart from her work in this field, she has interested herself in still life, figure and landscape. As may be seen in this drawing, she has always been concerned with formal structure, based on a cubistic manipulation of planes.

95. **Paraskeva Clark**
Across the Street, 1937. Pen and ink, 11⅞ x 9⅜ ins (45.4 x 23.8 cm). Collection: The National Gallery of Canada. Gift of the Douglas M. Duncan Collection, Toronto, 1970.

Regionalists

Carl Schaefer
1903–

A number of artists in the 1920s, possibly influenced by similar interests in the United States, turned to regional themes.

Among these were Carl Schaefer and André Biéler. Painting in the area of Hanover, Ontario, where he was born, Schaefer endowed his landscapes and farmhouse subjects with an intense sense of presence of the people who inhabited them, although the figures seldom appeared. In our drawing they are represented in a very effective decorative composition.

96. Carl Schaefer
Amish Couple at Heidelburg, Waterloo County,
1927. Pen and ink, 7¼ x 6½ ins (18.4 x 16.5 cm).
Private collection.

André Biéler
1896–

Biéler's paintings of rural families in Quebec endow them with a quiet dignity which reminds us of the peasant subjects produced by the brothers Le Nain in France in the seventeenth century.

97. André Biéler
Les deux vieux, St. Famille, I.O., 1927. Watercolor and conté, 9½ x 11 ins (24 x 27.9 cm).
Collection: The Agnes Etherington Art Centre.

Canadian Group of Painters

Jack Humphrey
1901–1967

In 1933 the Group of Seven was absorbed by a larger organization called the Canadian Group of Painters. The purpose was to widen the scope of both membership and regional representation. However, although the aim was similar to that proposed by the Contemporary Art Society in Montreal, the new group had to contend with the dominating influence of the senior founding members in order to strike out in new directions.

Humphrey was a member of this group. He studied in New York, Paris and Munich, and travelled extensively, but chose to spend his whole working life in Saint John.

This luminous drawing is a fine example of his New Brunswick landscapes.

98. Jack Humphrey
From Perry Point. Pencil with watercolor, 14½ x 21½ ins (36.7 x 54.6 cm). Collection: The National Gallery of Canada.

Three Independents

Alfred Pellan
1906–

Of more impact on the Canadian scene than the arrival of Brandtner in 1928 or Lyman in 1931 was the return of Pellan in 1940.

Brandtner had landed in an alien environment in Winnipeg, and was little heard from until his move to the East in 1934. Pellan, on the other hand, having spent fifteen years in Paris, came fresh from association with Picasso, Léger and Miró; and he brought with him a number of canvases which, when shown in Montreal, created a considerable sensation.

Of this exhibition Jacques de Tonnancour wrote: "What French Canadian art needed, in order to be resurrected after these centuries of lethargic slumber, was a vigorous blow from the outside and Pellan provided just that blow."

It was he who set in motion a revolution in the artist and student body in Montreal which finally led to the sweeping aside of academic restraints and the formation of groups such as the Automatistes and the Plasciciens.

Pellan, the individualist, belonged to none of these, but provided the initial momentum for change. In Paris his main affiliation was with the Surrealists, and that movement has remained one of the main sources of his powerful imagery throughout his career.

99. Alfred Pellan
Armuré. Graphite, 11¾ x 9 ins (29.8 x 22.9 cm).
Collection: The National Gallery of Canada.

David Milne
1882–1953

Two of Canada's greatest artists, Milne and Carr, were contemporaries of the Group of Seven.

Milne studied in New York and was represented in the famous Armory Show of 1913, which gave Americans their first comprehensive look at modern European art. During his New York period Milne's work bears a slight resemblance to that of his friend Maurice Prendergast; after that his statement became uniquely his own, so much so that he had no followers.

If one could choose one word to describe his method, it might be "economy." He never added a touch to a drawing or painting beyond the point where he considered that he had achieved his aim.

This early work already evinces his skill in energizing the white ground into defining the total space with the minimum amount of drawing.

100. **David Milne**
Bronx Hillside, 1915. Ink, 15 x 21 ins (38.1 x 53.3 cm). Collection: Mr. David P. Silcox, Toronto.

Emily Carr
1871–1945

Despite all the little human touches which embroider her life, known to us chiefly through her books, Carr has always seemed to me to be a heroic figure.

In the first place, she had to make her own way to get the training she needed; then she had to develop her art in an atmosphere of almost total incomprehension. Until she was "taken up" by Lawren Harris and made a member of the Canadian Group of Painters in 1933, she had resolutely to tread the path she had laid out for herself with no help and much frustration. In order to support herself she was obliged to almost give up painting during the years 1917–1928 while she tended a boarding house.

The contact late in life with other artists who appreciated her achievement was intoxicating, and led to her final flowering.

Like all artists Carr was subject to various influences. She had her early "Fauve" period after study in France; later her association with Mark Tobey and Lawren Harris affected her work. But it was the art of the West Coast Indians which had the greatest impact on her. Its formal characteristics helped to shape her own style, and its animistic spirit invested her forest subjects even when, at Harris' suggestion, she stopped painting Indian images.

Could this portrait of Jacob (Pl. 101) be the first depiction of a Canadian Indian child as being a normal member of the community, rather than some cute outgrowth of the papoose as presented by artists such as de Grandmaison?

101. Emily Carr
Jacob. Charcoal, 18¼ x 10⅜ ins (36.3 x 26.3 cm).
Collection: The Provincial Archives, Victoria, B.C.

102. Emily Carr
Tree Forms, c.1940. Oil on paper, 14⅝ x 10⅝ ins
(37 x 27 cm). The McMichael Canadian Collection, Kleinburg, Ontario.

Automatistes

Paul-Émile Borduas
1905–1960

The 1940s were turbulent years in Quebec. That Borduas and his friends were involved in revolutionary politics is evident from the manifesto *Refus Global* published in 1948. This was the culmination of the struggle against academic officialdom sparked by Pellan's return to Canada in 1940. It resulted in Borduas' dismissal from the teaching staff of L'École du Meuble. In the same year the Contemporary Art Society, of which Borduas was president, was dissolved due to internal dissentions.

The "Automatistes," as his group came to be known after their 1947 exhibition, were dedicated to Non-Objective art of a completely spontaneous unpremeditated kind. The aim can best be expressed in one sentence from *Refus Global:* "Refus de toute INTENTION, arme néfaste de la RAISON."

Of course, the source of the movement was Surrealism. It is interesting that Borduas, like so many other modern artists, was fascinated by child art and arranged exhibitions of it. This may explain another call in his manifesto— "Place à la Magie!"

103. Paul-Émile Borduas (left)
Sans titre, 1943. Mine de plomb, fusain, encre, lavis sur papier, 22⅗ x 20¼ ins (57.5 x 51.5 cm). Collection: Museum of Contemporary Art, Montreal.

104. Paul-Émile Borduas (below)
La Plante Héroique, 1950. Colored inks, 8¼ x 10¾ ins (21 x 27.3 cm). Collection: Art Gallery of Ontario. Gift of The J. S. McLean Collection. On loan to the Art Gallery of Ontario from the Ontario Heritage Foundation, 1970.

Léon Bellefleur
1910–

Surrealism was the primal source guiding the direction taken by the Automatistes, their pupils and followers. It was the key to their liberation from the disciplines of the past.

The intimate lyricism of Bellefleur's drawing is reminiscent of the works of Paul Klee.

105. Léon Bellefleur
Feux Follets, 1956. Ink and woodpoint, 15 x 12$^{11}/_{16}$ ins (38.1 x 32.2 cm). Collection: The National Gallery of Canada.

Guido Molinari
1933–

In 1957, with Leduc and Tousignant, Molinari allied himself with a group called *Les Plasticiens*.

It is evident, however, from this 1954 drawing that he was first influenced by the Automatistes.

106. Guido Molinari
Untitled, 1954. Pen and ink, 10 x 13⅛ ins (25.4 x 33.3 cm). Collection: The National Gallery of Canada.

Jean-Paul Riopelle
1923–

In his youth Riopelle was associated with the Automatistes, although he had moved to Paris in 1947, before the publication of *Refus Global*. Shortly thereafter he severed his connection with the group.

Riopelle's work has always been based on nature; forms and forces interpreted in gestural painting. Already in this early work it is possible to detect a close affiliation with the "action painting" of the New York School of the 1950s.

107. Jean-Paul Riopelle
Sans titre, 1946. Ink and watercolor, 11½ x 17 ins (29.2 x 43.2 cm). Collection: Mira Godard Gallery, Toronto.

West Coast

Jack L. Shadbolt
1909–

Emily Carr set herself down before the trees and transformed them into living emblems. After her no artist could go into the forests of British Columbia to paint without inviting comparison with her work.

They could, however, continue to seek in nature forms which could be used to symbolize aspects of human experience or consciousness.

Two of these were the West Coast painters Shadbolt and Jarvis.

In "Painting in Process," *Art and Artist*, University of California Press, Shadbolt stated: "To me a nature cycle—phases of seed growth, flowering, withering and dying of plants—is an apt paraphrase of the human cycle. . . ."

108. Jack L. Shadbolt
Presences after Fire. Ink and casein, 26¼ x 36¼ ins (66.7 x 92 cm). Collection: The National Gallery of Canada.

Donald Jarvis
1923–

The emblematic character of this drawing (Pl. 109) is evident.

The tangled natural forms convey a sense of emerging energy frustrated in a struggle for release. It was also in the 1950s that these turbulent forms underwent a metamorphosis into human figures in Jarvis' work (Pl. 110).

109. Donald Jarvis
Tangled Growth, 1953. Watercolor, 14½ x 10½ ins (36.7 x 26.7 cm). Collection: National Gallery of Canada.

110. Donald Jarvis
Two Figures, 1953. Watercolor, 14½ x 10½ ins (36.7 x 26.7 cm). Private collection.

B. C. Binning
1909–1976

Like Shadbolt and Jarvis (see Pls. 108-110), Binning was on the teaching staff of the Vancouver School of Art. He is best known for his drawings which reflect a quizzical but affectionate view of the life style of middle-class Van-couverites, particularly the boating community. West Coast artists holding teaching jobs were able to partake of this good life and, sponsored by the much revered Lawren Harris, were well integrated into local society.

111. B. C. Binning
Arbutus Tree, 1945. Ink, 17½ x 23½ ins (44.5 x 59.7 cm). Collection: The Art Gallery of Ontario.

War

Charles Goldhamer
1903–

The two World Wars raised, confirmed and established Canada's position as an identifiable, independent nation. Despite this, there appears to be a tendency to suppress the memory of these traumas.

Most of the works of official war artists on display in Ottawa are set pieces painted after the events they portray. The most vital records are the works on paper done in the field; these are hidden away in storage cabinets.

I have chosen one by Goldhamer to form a link with the psychological scars which we shall encounter later in contemporary works.

After the last war there is no need to pursue the historical method any further. Granted, the course of the mainstream, beloved of formalist critics, continued to be identifiable for another generation as it made its urgent way through Abstract Expressionism, Post-Painterly Abstracts and other developments until it disappeared into the sands of the delta. Today everything is not only possible, but acceptable—from Body Art to the New Realism.

From here on, drawings will be grouped, not to categorize the artist or the works in question, but to suggest a context in which to consider and enjoy them.

However, there remain two post-war exhibiting bodies which must be dealt with as entities—Les Plasticiens in Montreal and Painters Eleven in Toronto.

In 1955 a group of artists in Montreal calling themselves Plasticiens offered an alternative to automatism. They issued a manifesto calling for "the revelation of perfect forms in a perfect order." The nature of their abstracts precluded elements of drawing.

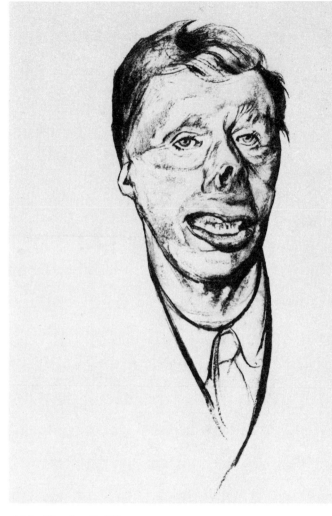

112. Charles Goldhamer
Burnt Airman. Charcoal, 14¼ x 14½ ins (36.2 x 36.7 cm). Collection: Canadian War Museums, Ottawa.

Painters Eleven

In 1953 a number of artists in Toronto, exasperated by the limited opportunities to show their work, decided to combine their efforts to promote group exhibitions for their members.

Painters Eleven, as they called themselves, held their first exhibition in 1954. Most of them were abstract painters whose interests were directed to New York, rather than Paris, which still retained the allegiance of their Montreal contemporaries.

Among those members of Painters Eleven who constituted the first generation of Canadian "Abstract Expressionists," Hodgson, Ronald and Town are represented in this book under various headings because their drawings, unlike their paintings, are not always Non-Objective.

J. W. G. (Jock) Macdonald
1897–1960

Jock Macdonald was the senior associate of Painters Eleven. A gifted teacher, he had been the instructor of some of the junior members.

In the last years of his life, stimulated by the group's activities, he achieved a breakthrough to a personal lyrical Non-Objective style. Previously he had experimented in several directions.

Our drawing is an example of a series he called "modalities," which closely paralleled Kandinsky's "improvisations."

113. J. W. G. Macdonald
Untitled, 1945. Watercolor, 9⅝ x 13⁹⁄₁₆ ins
(24.4 x 34.4 cm). Private collection, Toronto.

Alexandra Luke
1901–1967

This early drawing was done while Luke was still under the influence of her teacher Jock Macdonald.

At his suggestion, his students practiced automatic drawing. This work of Luke's might easily be thought to be by one of the Automatistes.

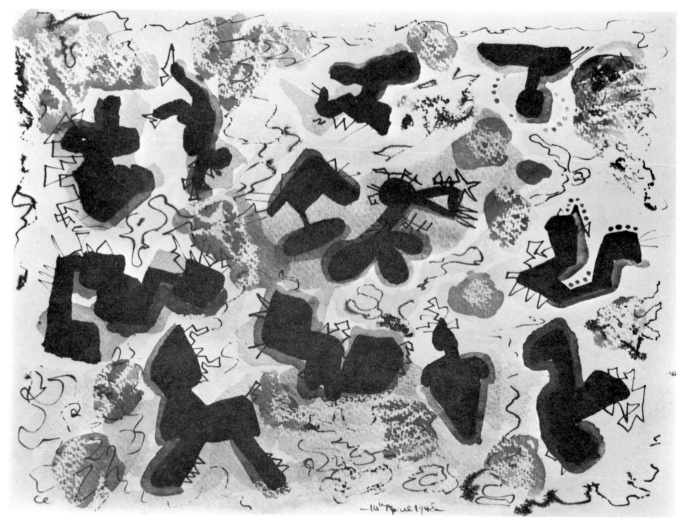

114. Alexandra Luke
Untitled, 1948. Ink and watercolor, 9 x 12 ins (22.9 x 30.4 cm). Collection: The Robert McLaughlin Gallery, Oshawa. Gift of Mr. and Mrs. E. R. S. McLaughlin, 1971.

Oscar Cahen
1916–1956

This drawing is as close as a graphic work can get to Abstract Expressionist painting.

Although it retains suggestions of surrealist images, its form is open and gestural.

Cahen studied in Europe and was twenty-four years old when he emigrated to Canada in 1940. Because of his European experience and age he was regarded with respect by other members of the group, most of whom were ten years younger than he.

115. Oscar Cahen
Drawing G182-2. Black, white and brown ink, 24⅞ x 38⅜ ins (63.1 x 97.5 cm). Collection: Art Gallery of Ontario. Gift from the McLean Foundation, 1964.

Ray Mead
1921–

The images which appear in this work are typical of those which occur frequently in the transitional period between Surrealism and Abstract Expressionism, which characterized the early works of Painters Eleven. (See also Pl. 113). Later, under the influence of New York artists such as Hans Hofmann, these images were submerged.

Like most members of Painters Eleven, Mead found support in commercial art. He was Art Director of MacLaren's in Toronto until 1957 when he moved to Montreal for the same firm.

After Cahen's death and Ronald's resignation the group dissolved in 1960 and each artist went his own way.

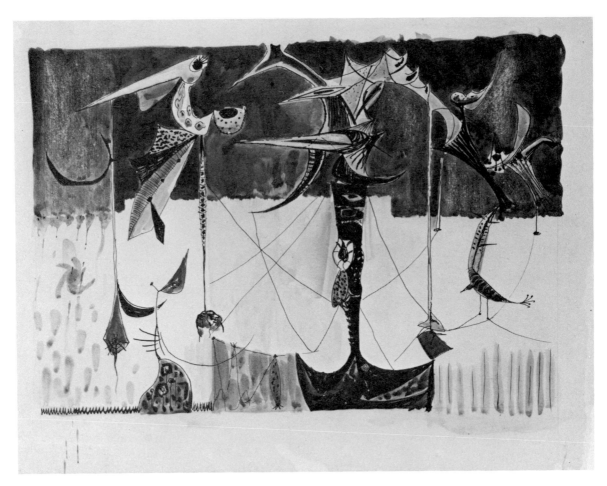

116. Ray Mead
Winter Garden No. 2, c.1952. Ink and graphite, 14¼ x 17¾ ins (36.2 x 45 cm). Collection: The Robert McLaughlin Gallery, Oshawa. On permanent loan from the Ontario Heritage Foundation, gift of M. F. Feheley, 1971.

Disquiet

Physiognomy has always been regarded as a reflection of character, and the eyes as a mirror of the soul. In art, basic extremes are represented by the masks of tragedy (the hero and the villain), and comedy (the wit and the buffoon).

But artists have also been interested in the abnormal. One thinks of the grotesques of Leonardo da Vinci, the *Disparates* of Goya, the studies of lunatics by Géricault, and the phantasmagorias of the Symbolists. Modern artists have distorted the face for formal reasons (Picasso, for instance) or for expressive purposes (in fact, all the Expressionists).

Instead of the physical wreckage brought about by war (Pl. 112) artists are now concerned with psychological wounds.

Claude Breeze
1938–

If we cover the right side of this face we are confronted with an image of terror; cover the left side, and we are conscious of manic glee. Viewed as a whole the drawing is a brilliant representation of schizophrenia.

117. Claude Breeze
Head #5, 1965. Ink, 18 x 12 ins (45.7 x 30.5 cm).
Collection: Miss Amy Smith.

Ivan Eyre
1935–

This drawing is one of a series included in Eyre's most recent exhibition. The bandaged heads do not conceal physical wounds, but suggest metaphorically men trapped in alienation, looking out fearfully at the world.

In many of his paintings the environment of their settings seems to portend disaster.

118. Ivan Eyre
Wrapped Head IV, 1978. Charcoal, 13 x 10 ins (33 x 25.3 cm). Collection: Mira Godard Gallery, Toronto.

Glenn Howarth
1946–

This drawing should be compared with the Binning (Pl. 111). It presents a very different perspective of waterfront users. Apparently Wreck Beach in Vancouver was the preserve of nude bathers, and the violence implicit in this savage apparition is in stark contrast to the comfortable world of Binning.

119. Glenn Howarth
Study for a Wreck Beach Nude, 1973. Ink, 11 x 5 ins (27.9 x 12.7 cm). Collection: The artist, courtesy The Bau-Xi Gallery, Toronto.

Shizueye Takashima
1928–

The 1960s were indeed a time of searching. Kennedy assumed office in 1961 and instigated the space program, the Peace Corps and the Alliance for Progress. But the U.S., recently embarrassed by the Bay of Pigs Invasion, was becoming increasingly involved in Southeast Asia, and with troubles in its own South. It was the time of the Freedom Riders. We have seen how artists reacted to the social problems of the 1930s; they were equally responsive to the stirrings of the 1960s.

Takashima's drawing is related to a series of paintings she was working on at the time, depicting judges as threatening figures. In it there are also echoes of Chadwick's series of sculptures titled "Watchers."

120. **Shizueye Takashima**
Men Searching, 1962. Ink, 18 x 24 ins (45.7 x 61 cm). Collection: The artist, courtesy The Loranger Gallery, Toronto.

The Analysis of Beauty

Leonardo da Vinci and Vitruvius sought to arrive at an understanding of the Greek ideal of beauty by analyzing the human figure in terms of geometry. To do this they drew it in the frame of the rectangle and circle. Later Hogarth published his *Analysis of Beauty*, using the same method in his diagrams.

Tony Urquhart
1934–

Urquhart obviously had these experiments in mind when he produced his series "The Men of Numbers." However, instead of analyzing the human figure, he presents man as victim, spayed, not for measurement, but as if suffering constraint.

121. **Tony Urquhart**
The Men of Numbers—Version No. 2, 1964. Ink and wash, $17^{13}/_{16} \times 6^{3}/_{16}$ ins (43.7 x 15.7 cm). Collection: Art Gallery of Ontario. Gift from the Georgia J. Weldon Estate, 1965.

Alex Colville
1920–

The purpose of Leonardo, Vitruvius and Hogarth was to seek a mathematical formula for the structure of an ideal figure. Colville, on the other hand, draws his figure and then proceeds to analyze it mathematically without changing his original perception.

If one examines three studies of the same subject one finds that the circles, radiating lines and squares he imposes on his drawings are not used for compositional purposes, because the disposition of forms hardly changes from version to version.

One can only assume that the geometric analysis he makes aids him in some way to understand the space his figures occupy, the better to define it in his final painting.

It would be hard to think of any artist more distrustful of facility than Colville.

122. **Alex Colville**
Study for Berlin Bus, 1978. Ink, 9 x 8¾ ins (22.9 x 22.2 cm). Collection: Mira Godard Gallery, Toronto.

Tom Hodgson
1924–

Talking of facility, Tom Hodgson, a Non-Objective painter, in looking over some of his recent drawings, decided that they were too "clever." So he devised a method of drawing from the model with a pen in each hand, using both simultaneously (the signature was made in the same way).

The result, as seen here, has a kind of satisfying toughness.

123. Tom Hodgson
Nude Studies. Ink, 12 x 8¾ ins each (30.5 x 22.2 cm). Collection: the artist.

Introverts

The three artists represented in this section all suffered periods of desperation in their private lives. One of them attempted suicide and the other two took their own lives. From their solitudes they reached out through the medium of their art.

William Kurelek
1927–1977

Kurelek became deeply religious, and much of his art attempts to proseletize. However, his earlier works record memories of his life on the prairies. Our drawing conveys a sense of solemnity and stillness, endowing a pioneer barn with something of the character of a nave.

124. William Kurelek
Manitoba Barn. Sepia ink, 21½ x 13 ins (54.6 x 33 cm). Collection: Mr. and Mrs. Christopher Ondaatje, Toronto.

Christine Pflug
1936–1972

If one did not know that this drawing is a self-portrait, one would take it to be a Symbolist work, expressing the tragic isolation of a withdrawn personality. Indeed it has much to say about Pflug's unhappy life.

125. Christine Pflug
Self-Portrait in a Window Pane, 1961. Pencil, 12½ x 9½ ins (31.7 x 24 cm). Collection: The Agnes Etherington Art Centre. Gift of Ayala and Samuel Zacks, 1962.

Richard Ciccimarra
1924–1973

A characteristic of Ciccimarra's work is a quiet
sense of tragedy—not the rage of the Expressionists, but the acceptance of a fatalist.

In this drawing defeat is personified in the
fallen figure.

126. Richard Ciccimarra
Five Figures. Conté and wash, 13 x 15 ins (33 x
38.1 cm). Collection: The Bau-Xi Gallery,
Toronto.

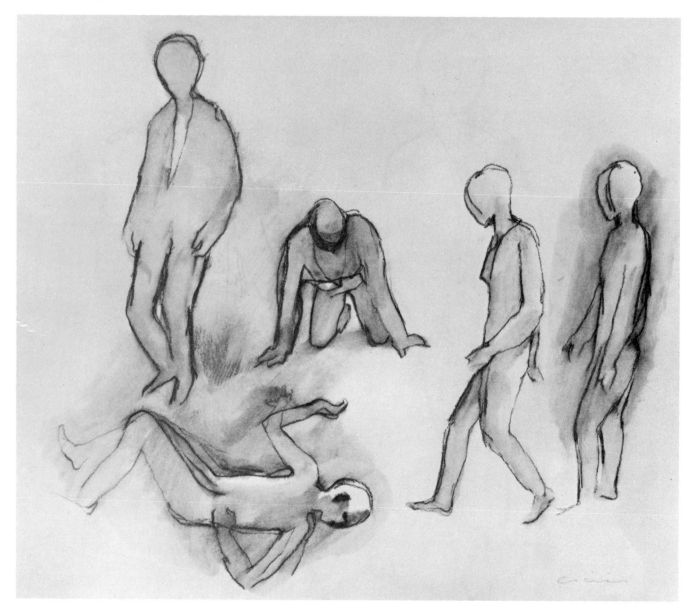

Extroverts

Extroverts involve themselves with life in all its manifestations—loving or hating with equal passion. In art intense feelings invite violent technique.

When I first came to Ontario some forty years ago, I found the climate of public opinion to be puritanical and inimical to any extravagance of expression. Even today, the high period of European Expressionist art, around the turn of the century, is poorly represented in our public collections.

However, since the 1950s our own extroverts have gained acceptance.

William Ronald
1926–

A founding member of Painters Eleven, Ronald has continued to paint in the Abstract Expressionist style. Resisting the temptation to fall in with subsequent developments in painting, he has stuck to the one which becomes him best.

Images were always lurking beneath the paint of the Abstract Expressionists, and in this drawing Ronald has allowed a powerful one to emerge.

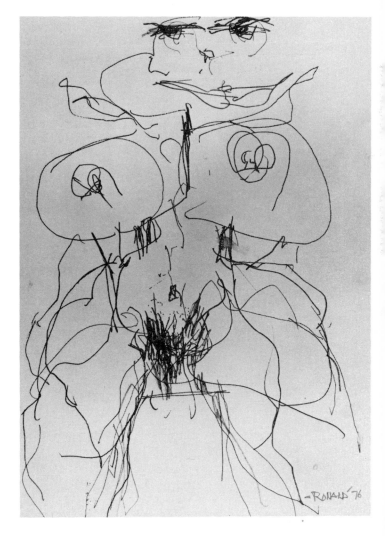

127. William Ronald
Nude, 1976. Colored inks, 29 x 21½ ins (73.6 x 54.6 cm). Collection: the artist.

Bruno Bobak
1923–

Bobak is a direct descendant of the German Expressionists. This powerful drawing reflects the compassionate interest he brings to all his studies of the human figure.

128. **Bruno Bobak**
Seated Nude. Ink and wash, 24 x 18½ ins (61 x 47 cm). Collection: the artist.

Robert Markle
1936–

The Falling Figure drawings are related to a
series Markle painted on strippers in the 1960s.
This interest in burlesque has been shared by
many artists who probably recognize in the per-
formers practitioners of another art or ritual.

   As may be seen, Markle's approach to the
subject was sensuous but not erotic.

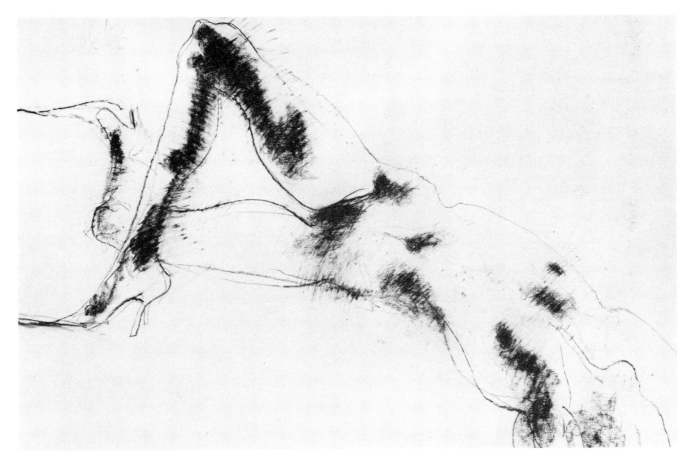

129. Robert Markle
Falling Figure, 1966. Charcoal, 23¼ x 35 ins
(59 x 89 cm). Collection: the artist, courtesy
The Isaacs Gallery, Toronto.

Mashel Teitelbaum
1921–

This drawing should properly be in the portrait section of this book. However, it is handled with such a bold Fauve attack that I have included it with other expressionist works.

It is not generally realized that many self-portraits have resulted from an artist's desire to work at a time when no other model offered itself.

130. **Mashel Teitelbaum**
Self Portrait as Rembrandt, 1979. Pencil and acrylic, 14 x 16¾ ins (35.5 x 42.5 cm). Collection: Mr. R. McCrea, Toronto.

Correlations No. 1
Form and Space

Stanley Lewis
1930–

Lewis uses a monumental sculptural form which, in its dead weight extension on the earth, eloquently expresses a sense of hopelessness. We are very conscious of the ground.

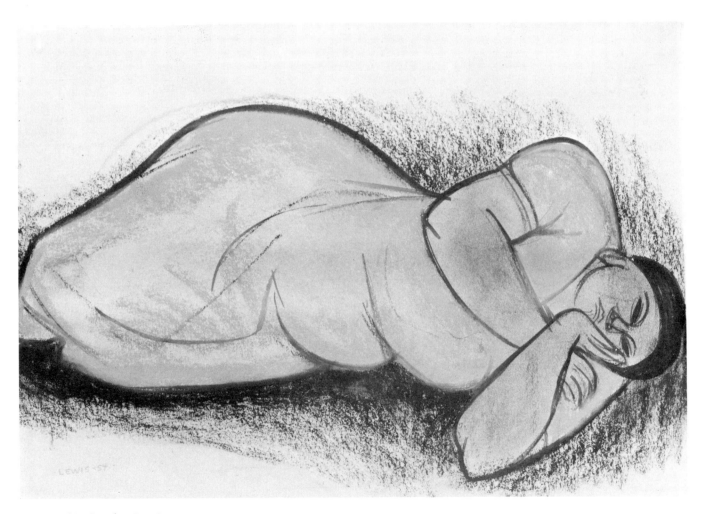

131. Stanley Lewis
Reclining Figure, 1954. Chalk and wash, 18¾ x 26¾ ins (47.6 x 67.9 cm). Collection: The Montreal Museum of Fine Arts.

Anne Kahane
1924–

Kahane, on the other hand, has chosen an open structure in her series of the Seasons, in which the figures are permeated by the surrounding space. In this case, it is the air around and beyond the figures of which we are aware, rather than the ground.

132. **Anne Kahane**
June '58, 1958. Pen and ink, 28⅝ x 22½ ins (72.7 x 57.1 cm). Collection: Art Gallery of Ontario. Canada Council Joint Drawings Purchase Fund, 1961.

Correlations No. 2
Nudes: Romantic/Classic

Peter Harris
1932–

Harris is best known for his paintings of women. He does not use a model. As he has said: "Instead of painting a particular woman, you paint all women." This is a romantic approach, indicating his love of the subject. It does not imply that the results are sentimental; on the contrary, his form is vigorous.

133. Peter Harris
Olympia VI, 1972. Oil and pastel on paper, 24 x 32 ins (61 x 81.2 cm). Collection: the artist.

Christopher Pratt
1935–

Pratt is generally categorized as a realist. However, his drawings, with their insistent line, suggest a classical approach, seeking an ideal rather than a real form.

134. Christopher Pratt
Two Nude Studies, 1974. Pencil, 10½ x 10½ ins
(26.7 x 26.7 cm). Collection: Mr. and Mrs.
Christopher Ondaatje, Toronto.

Correlations No. 3
Animate and Inanimate Objects: Impressionist/Realist

Paul Fournier
1939–

Fournier's study, with its placement on the page, has some resemblance to a French rococo decorative panel. It also recalls the still life paintings of Renoir, who was influenced by French eighteenth century art. It is certainly handled in an impressionist manner.

135. Paul Fournier
Mushroom Series No. 12, 1972. Ink and wash, 24¼ x 36 ins (62.2 x 91.4 cm). Collection: Art Gallery of Ontario.

Ken Nutt
1951–

This drawing has affinities with a particular kind of realism called "trompe l'oeil." In works of this genre the artists painted casual arrangements of still life objects in such a way as to "deceive the eye" into thinking they are real.

Obviously this is not Nutt's intention, but the loving care he has bestowed on his drawing reminds us of similar arrangements by the nineteenth century American trompe l'oeil artists Peto and Harnett.

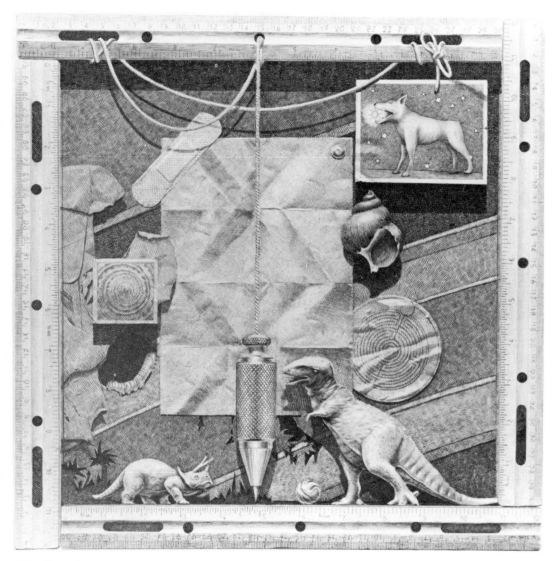

136. Ken Nutt
A Natural History (Wing of a triptych). Pencil and prisma color, 13¼ x 13¼ ins (33.6 x 33.6 cm).
Collection: the artist.

Correlations No. 4
Abstract Images: Tactile values

Gerald Gladstone
1929–

These two drawings, both of which contain wheel-like shapes, could have been compared on several levels. I have used tactility to emphasize their different qualities.

Gladstone's forms are hard and metalic, related to his galactic series of sculptures. They fill the space in an oppressive way which calls to mind the famous fantastic prison scenes of the eighteenth century artist Piranesi.

Meredith, on the other hand, deploys an open space, and his forms are slightly blurred and more biomorphic, resulting in a general feeling of lyricism (Pl. 138).

137. Gerald Gladstone
Drawing No. 71, 1961. Ink and brush, $10^{15}/_{16}$ x $14^{7}/_{8}$ ins (27.7 x 37.8 cm). Collection: Art Gallery of Ontario.

John Meredith
1933–

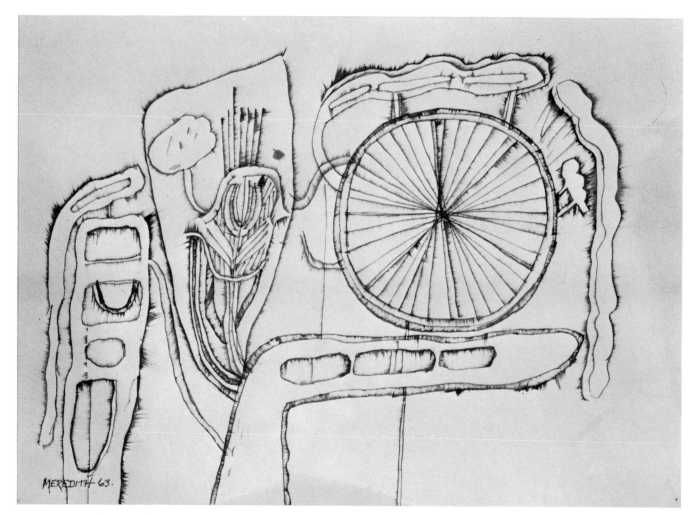

138. John Meredith
Untitled II, 1963. Pen and ink, 10½ x 14½ ins
(26.7 x 36.7 cm). Collection: Art Gallery of
Ontario.

Correlations No. 5
The Artist's Model:
Informal/Formal

Gordon Rice
1933–

One of the all-time classic subjects is the artist's model, usually in a studio setting, as is the case in both these drawings.

On Rice's page we have the model, the easel and, in place of the artist, a reclining figure, Ethel, who seems to fit comfortably into the scene.

Bashinski does bronze sculptures in which figures emerge in low relief from the background. In this very large drawing the figures are treated in a similar manner. Then, as if by afterthought, he has imposed sweeping Matisse-like lines which advance the forms towards the viewer (Pl. 140).

139. Gordon Rice
Ester in Alizerin, Model in Blue, 1975. Watercolor, 8¾ x 12 ins (22.2 x 30.5 cm). Collection: the artist.

Walter Bashinski
1939–

140. Walter Bashinski
Artist and Model, 1977. Pastel, 57 x 57 ins
(144.7 x 144.7 cm). Collection: the artist,
courtesy The Moos Gallery, Toronto.

Correlations No. 6
Geometric Forms:
Static/Dynamic

Leslie Poole
1942–

Artists are just as interested in Nature's geometry as in its biomorphic forms—a crystal is as much a subject for art as a vine.

Westerland's drawing is related to a series of concrete and steel wall structures which were the subject of her sculpture exhibition at the time. The full effect of the drawing is lost in reproduction because the texture is important. However, it is possible to see that the softening of the hard edges of the solid form release it somewhat into surrounding space (Pl. 142).

Poole's drawing is also one of a series, based on sail shapes. While Westerland has reduced a dense substance, Poole has solidified a slack one: the wall is given mobility, while the flapping sail is stilled. In both cases the artist's intention is architectural.

141. Leslie Poole
Shark Sail, 1977. Pencil, 25 x 34 ins (63.5 x 86.3 cm). Collection: the artist, courtesy The Bau-Xi Gallery, Toronto.

Mia Westerland
1942–

142. Mia Westerland
Untitled, 1977. Pastel, 28¼ x 24 ins (71.7 x
61 cm). Collection: the artist, courtesy The Sable
Gallery, Toronto.

Correlations No. 7
Forms Defining Space: Closed/Open

Frank Nulf
1931–

In Nulf's drawing we again have one of a series: this time related to beam-like shapes. In this case the artist seems to be insisting on the reality and presence of his modules—or what the philosophers like to call phenomenology. The space is claustrophobic.

At the opposite extreme, Zuck's space speeds to infinity, the rectangular shape serving as a way-station. Above hovers a cloud-like shape adding dimension to the space. The combination of the two forms induces a haunting quality in the drawing (Pl. 144).

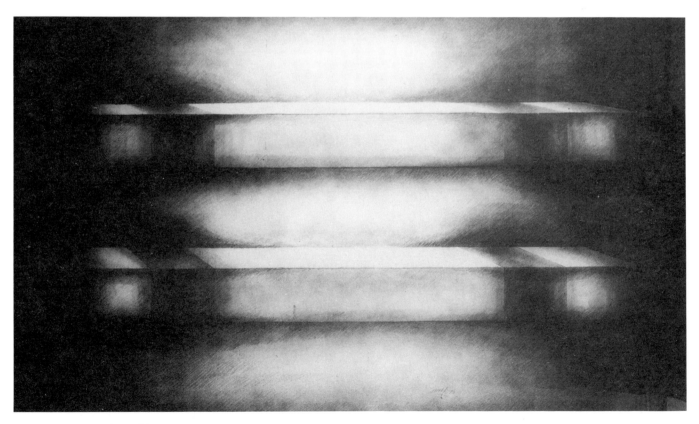

143. Frank Nulf
Two Warm Boxes, 1978. Graphite and watercolor, 42 x 70 ins (106.7 x 177.8 cm). Collection: the artist, courtesy The Bau-Xi Gallery, Toronto.

Tim Zuck
1947–

144. Tim Zuck
No. 105, 1979. Charcoal and graphite, 20 x 20 ins
(50.8 x 50.8 cm). Collection: Mrs. E. L. Stringer,
Toronto.

Figures

Aba Bayefsky
1923–

Since the turn of the century, when a group of artists known as the Ashcan School turned their attention to the activities of common folk in New York, many artists have recognized that the main problems of our time are social and, to a large extent, focused in the cities.

Bayefsky's art has always concerned itself with the human condition. Our drawing is one of a long series he made in the Kensington Market, Toronto.

145. **Aba Bayefsky**
Vegetable Stall, 1975. Pencil,
7¾ x 5¼ ins (19.7 x 13.3 cm).
Collection: the artist.

Gary Michael Dault
1939–

One's first impression of this drawing is that it is monumental. However one soon discovers that the central form is penetrated at its extremeties, and the eye, guided by the artist, is led on a swift tour of the edges to the corners of the picture.

The result is a work which combines simplicity with complexity, and monumentality with openness.

146. Gary Michael Dault
Dancer, 1979. Ink and wash, 25½ x 20 ins (64.8 x 50.8 cm). Collection: the artist.

Maxwell Bates
1906–

Because puppets are characterizations as visualized by the artist, I have included Bates' gesticulating group in this section. As a matter of fact, many of the figures in his paintings have the appearance of puppets, and are not unlike those crowding the fantasies of the Belgian painter James Ensor.

In our drawing each puppet seems to be absorbed in its own private action, regardless of the others on stage.

147. Maxwell Bates
Puppets, 1974. Ink and watercolor, 14⅛ x 20 ins
(35.9 x 50.8 cm). Collection: The Bau-Xi Gallery,
Toronto.

Charles Pachter
1942–

This drawing eloquently expresses the feeling one has after a busy day in a foreign city on return to one's hotel room—a sort of reflective, beaten-down ennui.

The scenario and perspective owe something to film.

148. Charles Pachter
David and Peter in Paris Hotel, 1979. Ink and dry brush on paper handmade by the artist, 19 x 25 ins (48.3 x 63.5 cm). Collection: the artist.

Jean-Paul Lemieux
1904–

Lemieux seems to have inherited some of the spirit of Ozias Leduc (see Pls. 52, 53) in the sense that they both distanced themselves from the hurly-burly of modern life and centered their interest on the Quebec rural scene.

Some may find this drawing to be too sen-timental for their taste, but the sentiment conveyed is a genuine feeling for the springtime of life. The contrast between the delicacy of the white figure and the textural background of trees is beautifully achieved.

149. Jean-Paul Lemieux
Untitled, 1973. Ink, 28 x 22 ins (71.1 x 55.8 cm).
Collection: the artist.

Portraits

Before the invention of photography artists could expect that a considerable proportion of their patronage would depend on portrait commissions, particularly at the start of their careers before they had developed a market for their own preferred subject matter. Indeed, there have been periods when portraits were the only works in demand—for example, in colonial America, or in eighteenth century England, when wealthy collectors were scrambling for Italian seicento paintings, leaving artists such as Romney and Gainsborough to complain about the drudgery of "face-painting" which fell to their lot.

Photography has relieved artists of much of the hack work, and freed them for a more creative approach to portraiture.

Dorothy Stevens
1888–1966

This drawing by Dorothy Stevens is a study of the kind which calls for intensive concentration by the artist in the presence of the sitter, and conveys to the viewer an impression of intimate recognition.

Stevens was one of Canada's finest etchers and her work in this medium is too seldom seen.

150. **Dorothy Stevens**
Portrait. Pencil, 10¼ x 10¼ ins (26 x 26 cm). Private collection.

Dennis Burton
1933–

Burton's portrait is as masterly as that of Stevens, but more stylish—by that I mean that he has injected more of his own manner into the work.

In one case one thinks of a work of art by a skilled portrait painter (Pl. 150); in the other (Pl. 151) one thinks of an artist drawn by a compulsive wish to make a portrait.

151. Dennis Burton
Portrait of Malka Fry, 1964. Pencil, 16¾ x 15 ins (42.5 x 38.1 cm). Collection: the artist, courtesy The Isaacs Gallery, Toronto.

Hugh Mackenzie
1928–

The "Mackenzie" is a working drawing for a commissioned portrait. It is a good demonstration that, although in such cases the artist's primary concern may be to capture a "likeness," his talents can be strong enough to supervene, with the result that a genuine work of art is produced.

152. Hugh Mackenzie
Study for the Portrait of Dr. Ross Mackenzie,
1974. Pencil, squared, 8 x 6 ins (20.3 x 15.2 cm).
Private collection.

Gordon Rayner
1935–

Like all self-portraits, this splendid drawing has an air of drama. The addition of the tape is interesting. It both establishes the picture surface and, probably, satisfies Rayner's fondness for collage as a means of confronting the abstract with the real. In this connection, one thinks of Rauschenberg as a possible source.

153. Gordon Rayner
Self-Portrait, 1972. Pencil and tape on paper, 13½ x 10½ ins (34.2 x 26.6 cm). Collection: the artist, courtesy The Isaacs Gallery, Toronto.

Narrative

David Blackwood
1941–

Narrative painting, both historical and contemporary, reached the height of its popularity in the Victorian Age. Its function has now largely been usurped by the camera, and those artists who continue to pursue it are usually primitives.

Blackwood, like Kurelek, is an exception. He has made many paintings describing the life of the east coast seamen. Our drawing was made to commemorate the passing of Wesleyville's last great ice captain. Captain Lew was a veteran of forty-five years in the Labrador Sea, a fishing skipper in arctic ice under sail. He spent the same number of springs at the icefields as a sealing captain.

154. David Blackwood
Captain Lew Kean passing, 1978. Pencil, 22 x 28 ins (55.9 x 71 cm). Collection: Gallery Pascal, Toronto.

Landscape

The long tradition of landscape painting in Canada continues. Although some artists, such as de Tonnancour and Nakamura who brought a fresh approach to the subject have, at least for the present, abandoned it, there will always be others to take their place. After all, it can hardly be ignored—especially in Canada.

Dorothy Knowles
1927–

The landscapes of Knowles afford evidence that the Impressionist vision survives. The discontinuous strokes with which she builds her scenes admit light to saturate them.

155. Dorothy Knowles
Wheatfield in June, 1976. Charcoal, 21 x 29½ ins (53.5 x 74.9 cm). Private collection.

Ann Kipling
1934–

Kipling is one of a number of "independents" in British Columbia, following their own course unheeding of any contemporary trends.

Our drawing is one of a series of small works she has recently done in the high country near Falkland. Instead of proceeding from the general to the particular, she works in the opposite direction, moving from detail to detail until she has achieved a satisfying whole.

Kipling's landscape drawings convey a sense of reverence for living things which one finds in medieval art.

156. Ann Kipling
Falkland Landscape, 1978. Pencil, 5⅜ x 7⅛ ins (13.7 x 18 cm). Collection: Mr. Chris Varley.

Takao Tanabe
1926–

Tanabe here achieves a dramatic effect by tonal contrast between the arching sky and the dark stillness of the hills.

157. Takao Tanabe
Prairie Hills, c.1979. Graphite, 27½ x 39½ ins (69.9 x 100 cm). Collection: the artist, courtesy The Glenbow Foundation, Calgary.

Gordon A. Smith
1919–

In Smith's drawing we are also conscious of vastness. Tanabe achieved the effect by contrasts of tone and texture, Smith employs planar perspective intensified by the faint cloud line on the horizon.

158. Gordon A. Smith
Landscape. Ink, 7¾ x 9¾ ins (19.7 x 24.7 cm).
Private collection.

Kazuo Nakamura
1926–

This drawing was done two years before the
foundation of Painters Eleven, of which Nakamura was a member. It demonstrates the strong
attraction which Abstract Expressionism exerted
on all members of the group at that time.

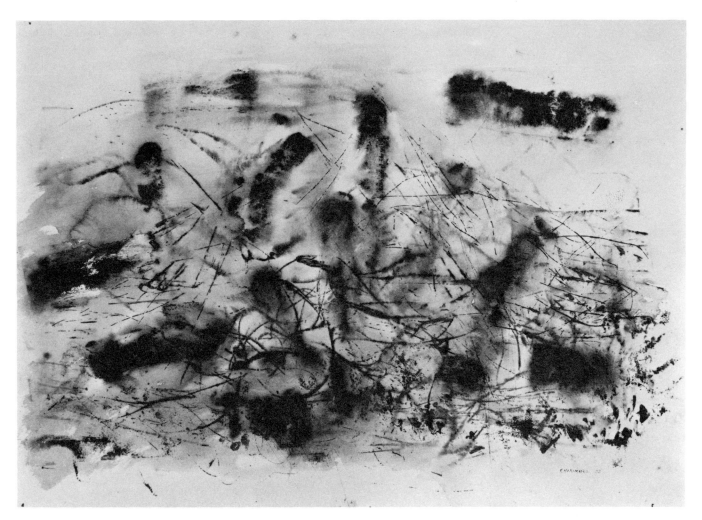

159. Kazuo Nakamura
Landscape, 1952. Watercolor and ink, 14²/₃ x
20½ ins (37.8 x 52.4 cm). Collection: The Robert
McLaughlin Gallery, Oshawa.

Dreams and Fantasies

Kenneth Lochhead
1926–

Surrealism has had an all-pervasive influence on much of the art of this century, both Non-Objective and figurative.

Lochhead's powerful drawing strikes echoes of de Chirico and Picasso. Most figurative artists, at some period of their development, have had to work their way through the cornucopia of ideas opened up by the latter.

Lochhead is now a Non-Objective painter.

160. **Kenneth Lochhead**
Dream, 1957. Pastel, 23 x 18 ins (58.4 x 45.7 cm). Private collection.

Jean Dallaire
1916–1965

This Surrealist work is as spritely as a Miró, but it was Lurçat who introduced Dallaire to the movement while he was in Paris studying with Maurice Denis and André Lhote in 1938.

Subsequently he worked for the National Film Board.

161. **Jean Dallaire**
Girl Weightlifting, 1960.
Mixed media, 15½ x
12⅜ ins (39.3 x 31.4 cm).
Collection: Mr. Simon
Dresdnere, Toronto.

Esther Warkov
1941–

Warkov also lingers in the realm of fantasy. In
this drawing she seems to be indulging a nostalgic
reverie about several generations in the history of
a family.

162. Esther Warkov
Family Reunion, c.1965. Pencil, 23 x 29 ins
(58.4 x 73.6 cm). Collection: Mr. David P. Silcox,
Toronto.

Diane Pugen
1943–

Were it not for the looming elephant, one might take this drawing for a modern version of the Fête Champêtre.

163. Diane Pugen
Elephantasy. Graphite and collage, 27 x 40 ins (69 x 10.1 cm). Collection: the artist.

Satire

Satire is a weapon which can only be wielded in free countries, which is why so much art is always suppressed by totalitarian regimes.

However, even in the Western democracies, little satirical art is produced today. Social and political protest has been transferred from the visual arts to pickets and marches.

Our time has called forth no Hogarth or Goya, nor even a George Grosz, all of whom dealt with specific instances of injustice or tyranny.

Louis de Niverville
1933–

Many of de Niverville's works have had a dream-like quality bordering on Surrealism; others seem to have been based on a recall of family life. In this particular series of drawings he portrayed various personalities with fantastic accessories (e.g. the alligator rug), brushing them with a gentle satiric touch.

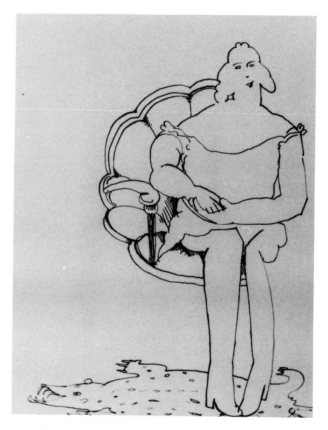

164. Louis de Niverville
Family Album Series: Seated Lady with Alligator Rug. Ink, 10¾ x 8¼ ins (27.3 x 21 cm).
Private collection, Toronto.

Florence Vale
1909–

In this drawing Vale seems to be satirizing the classical nude. Could this be an early manifestation of women's liberation?

Print drawings like this one are made by laying a sheet of paper on an inked lithographic stone and applying pressure on the paper surface with a sharp point. The image appears in reverse on the opposite side. The result is a combination of intention and fortuity.

165. **Florence Vale**
Nude, 1966. Unique print drawing, 11½ x 8½ ins (29 x 21.6 cm).
Private collection.

David James Gilhooly
1943–

This drawing could equally well have appeared under the heading "Fantasy"—but many works of fantasy contain a satirical element. Unlike Aesop, who also used animals to comment on human behavior, Gilhooly in his Frog Series does not moralize.

166. David James Gilhooly
The Honey Children, 1973. Ink, felt pen, 26½ x 36 ins (67.3 x 91.4 cm). Collection: Art Gallery of York University, Toronto.

Humor

One of the elements of satire is humor—rare in Canadian art.

Joyce Wieland
1931–

Wieland did a series in comic strip format depicting disasters of various kinds; liners sinking and aircraft crashing. In our drawing she substitutes a posturing figure for a plane, creating havoc and dismay in the inhabitants of the landscape.

167. Joyce Wieland
Flying, 1955. Ink, 9½ x 10¼ ins (24 x 26 cm).
Collection: Dr. Henry Levison, Toronto.

Hilda Woolnough
1934–

The subject of Woolnough's drawing is also flight unaided by mechanical means.

As in the case of the Wieland drawing, the humor is not unalloyed. In both these works there appear to be implications of comment on the idiocyncracies of human behavior.

168. Hilda Woolnough
Fat lady tries to fly, 1972. Ink, 19¾ x 14¼ ins (50.1 x 36.2 cm). Collection: Montreal Museum of Fine Arts. Purchased 1971 Horsley and Annie Townsend Bequest.

Parody

John MacGregor
1944–

Parody has always been one vehicle for the satirist—and, beyond him, the caricaturist.

It has also been a means of expressing admiration. MacGregor has here indulged himself in creating a charming version of Boucher's famous painting "Miss Murphy."

169. John MacGregor
Miss Murphy. Ink, pencil, pastel, 23⅛ x 29¼ ins (58.7 x 74.2 cm). Collection: the artist, courtesy The Isaacs Gallery, Toronto.

Variations on a Theme

Harold Town
1924–

Composers have often taken a theme from another's work to use as a basis for variations of their own (Rhapsody on a Theme of Paganini by Rachmaninoff, for instance). A drawing by Florence Vale (see Pl. 165) set Town off on an extraordinary series of variations, employing every resource of his art as the most prolific draughtsman of our time. From drawing to drawing technique, form and medium changed in a seemingly inexhaustible flow of inventiveness. Pl. 170 is the 212th.

In this example the white shapes look as if they had been scissored out.

170. Harold Town
Vale Variation #212, Pyramid of Roses, 1977. Ink, 28½ x 22½ ins (72.4 x 57.1 cm). Collection: the artist.

Signs and Symbols

Sorel Etrog
1933–

Etrog's abstract bronzes have always had an underlying reference to the human figure.

This page of studies, exploring ideas for sculpture, includes one which seems to refer to the pregnant woman series, and others relating to the twisted ribbon-like forms of the bronzes of the early 1960s.

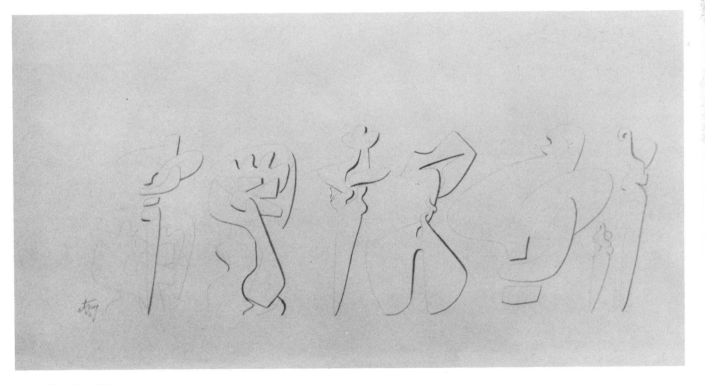

171. Sorel Etrog
Studies for Sculpture, 1962. Pencil, 12 x 20 ins (30.5 x 50.8 cm). Collection: Mr. Geert van der Veen, Toronto.

Tim Whiten
1941–

In recent years Whiten has been producing sculpture and assemblages based on the cult of fetish-
ism. Many of these have incorporated skulls,
which may have led him to the word Golgotha,
and hence this image.

172. Tim Whiten
Golgotha, 1978. Gold paint on handmade paper,
20 x 15½ ins (50.8 x 39.4 cm). Collection: the
artist.

Ronald Bloore
1925–

Bloore's drawings often suggest inscriptions or hieroglyphs from one of the ancient cultures which have engaged his interest.

One might take this drawing to be a cryptic representation of some hierarchy.

173. Ronald Bloore
Untitled, 1964. Colored inks, 13 x 20 ins (33 x 50.8 cm). Collection: Mr. David P. Silcox, Toronto.

"Scottie" Wilson
1890–1972

I have always felt that there was something of the pavement artist in "Scottie" Wilson. I do not mean this in any derogatory way, but only in the sense that he seems impelled by the need to fill all the available space with his graphic images, and that they are not so much symbolic as decorative.

174. "Scottie" Wilson
Untitled. Crayon and ink, 18½ x 9½ ins (47 x 24 cm). Collection: The Montreal Museum of Fine Arts. Gift of the Douglas M. Duncan Collection, 1970.

Primitives

Sindon Gecin
1907–

There are two kinds of primitives (or self-taught artists). One attempts to achieve professional standards and, in failing, produces works of charming naivete. The other makes no attempt to acquire traditional skills, and follows his own bent with the fresh vision of a child.

Gecin belongs to the latter group. In this drawing he pays homage to his great predecessor.

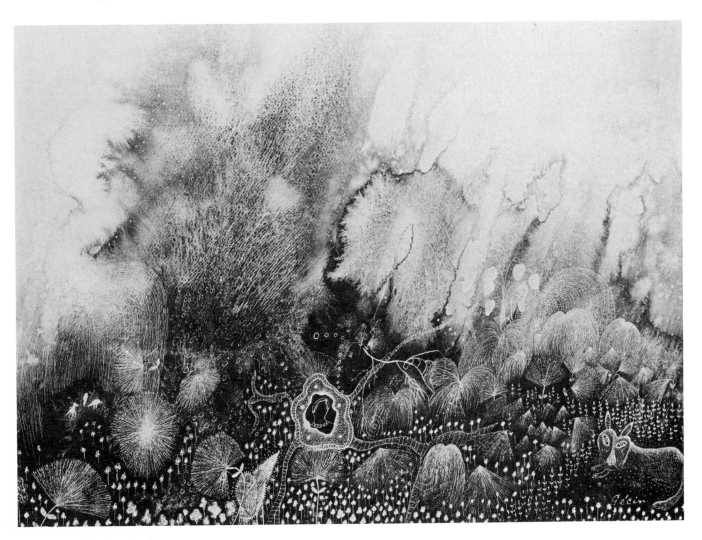

175. Sindon Gecin
Hommage à Henri Rousseau le Douanier, 1958.
Gouache and ink, 17½ x 23½ ins (44.5 x 59.7 cm).
Collection: Mr. Simon Dresdnere, Toronto.

Alma Rumball
1902–

The Rumball drawing is quite another case. It is recorded that about 1955 she received a mysterious impulse to translate to paper visions which came to her from an outside source. In a long series of drawings she responded to this call and produced her "automatic" works. This drawing is one of the earliest. We are in the realm of enchantment.

176. Alma Rumball
Cat No. 2, 1957. Colored inks, 17¼ x 12 ins (43.8 x 30.5 cm). Collection: the artist.

After Pop Art

Although Pop Art had a short life span, its influence on subsequent figurative art has been pervasive. As a movement it was timely in two senses. Firstly, it offered a solution to the problem of avoiding repetition of past styles by eliminating style—and, ironically, created a recognizable style of its own. Secondly, like the minimalists who came forth at the same time, it eschewed the autographic touch.

The drawings in this section, in one way or another, owe something to Pop Art.

John Boyle
1941–

The Pop element in Boyle's paintings consists of his introduction of well-known public figures (such as Lenin) into the surroundings of his home town, London, Ontario. In Pop, images of figures of universal familiarity were used on the same level as household appliances.

The difference is that Boyle has also represented less-known Canadian heroes, as in our drawing . . . not a bad way to promote the search for that illusive Canadian identity!

177. **John Boyle**
Chartrand. Ink on paper, 16½ x 20½ ins (42 x 52 cm). Collection: Dalhousie University Art Gallery, Halifax.

Christian Knudsen
1945–

In this drawing we are confronted with a double image, as in many of Warhol's works. Another Pop element is the depiction of a commonplace object—in this case a toilet bowl.

Although the seating accommodation is not as lethal, it is as depressing to the viewer as Warhol's electric chairs, which is a considerable achievement.

178. Christian Knudsen
Excusado. Photo emulsion on canvas board, 7 x 11⅔ ins (18 x 30 cm). Collection: The Canada Council Art Bank.

Arthur Boucher
1911–

The Pop element in this drawing lies in the employment by Boucher of what has become a national art-image, the Group of Seven uninhabited northern landscape. Into its solemn silence he has introduced a trio of noisy children.

179. Arthur Boucher
Group of Three, 1977. Ink and pastel, 10 x 9 ins (25.4 x 22.9 cm). Collection: the artist.

Aiko Suzuki
1939–

Aiko works primarily with fabrics to make wall-pieces, space dividers and hanging structures.

This drawing is only related to the work of the Pop artists by its inclusion of the coat hanger, a commonplace object typical of their iconography. In Aiko's hands, however, it attains a mystic significance rather than a brash reality.

180. Aiko Suzuki
Untitled, 1979. Acrylic, 23 x 18 ins (58.4 x 45.7 cm). Collection: the artist.

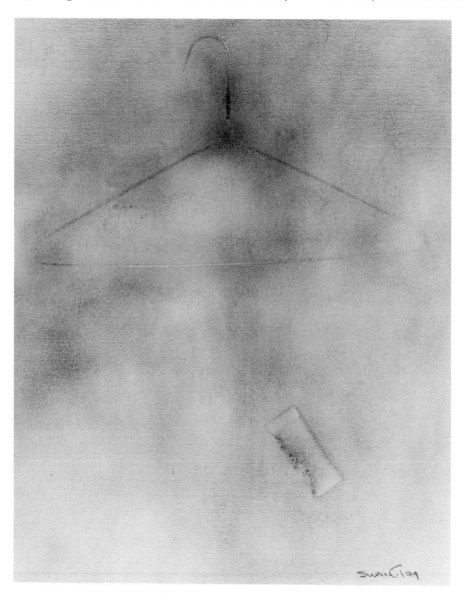

Mary Pratt
1935–

I have placed this drawing in this section to draw attention to a curious fact. Throughout art history still lifes including edible items have been a standard subject for artists. One thinks of the swags of fruit of the fifteenth century Paduan School, the bodegones of the seventeenth century Spaniard Zurbaran, the luscious piles of food of his Dutch contemporaries, and so on to the apples of Cézanne.

Artists have used these models either for decorative purposes, or to display their skills in realistic rendering, or as compositional elements. We have admired the pictures, but never thought of eating their content—until the arrival of Pop Art. This applies to examples as late as the Fitz-Gerald (Pl. 78) and the Fournier (Pl. 135) in this book. After Pop Art, however, in works by artists such as Oldenberg and Ramos, our taste buds have been tickled by eatable objects they have represented. Mary Pratt's "Meringue" is of this genre.

181. **Mary Pratt**
Meringue, 1978. Ink, 22 x 30 ins (55.8 x 76.2 cm). Collection: the artist, courtesy The Aggregation Gallery, Toronto.

Realism

This term, which used to mean "anti-ideal," has now come to designate various forms of painting which have been called "Magic, Super, or Photo-Realism." Because this has become the most popular genre in contemporary art, it has attracted artists of widely varying talent. Their productions range from the visual cliché to very serious attempts to explore metaphysics.

The most common element in all these works is time ... time-past (nostalgia) and time-present (awareness).

The latest manifestation has inevitably been called "New Realism." It is largely based on the transposition of photographic images into paintings with an obsessive exactitude. The intention is to present a candid image, devoid of subjective comment of any kind—not symbolic, nostalgic, poetic, anecdotal or emotional, but totally objective.

John Leonard
1944–

Although Leonard's paintings have a distinctly modern look, at times related to Pop Art, this drawing is a fine example of traditional realist art. It could have been done by any talented artist since the seventeenth century.

182. John Leonard
Studies of a Young Borzoi, 1979. Graphite, 29 x 23 ins (73.6 x 58.4 cm). Collection: the artist.

Ken Danby
1940–

Although it is not apparent in this working study, Danby is one of the leading exponents of the uncompromising New Realism.

183. Ken Danby
Working the Horse, 1975–76. Pencil, 17½ x
22¾ ins (44.5 x 57.8 cm). Private collection.

Realism: Gothic

The adjective Gothic is applied here not in the medieval sense, but as characterizing the literary trend of late eighteenth and early nineteenth century novels. A forerunner was Horace Walpole's *The Castle of Otranto*, 1764. Sir Christopher Wren described Gothic style as "tasteless, bizarre, rude, grotesque, romantic," while John Evelyn employed the terms "fantastical, licentious, full of fret and lamentable imagery." A typical artist of the period was Fuseli.

Tom La Pierre
1930–

We can find some of these qualities in this drawing. As the title suggests, it is sheer theatre. Whatever is taking place on the stage, the character of the drama is Gothic.

184. Tom La Pierre
Curtain Descending, 1973. Carbon pencil, 17½ x 28 ins (44.4 x 71 cm). Collection: the artist, courtesy The Prince Arthur Galleries, Toronto.

Eric Freifeld
1919–

In Freifeld's slowly maturing drawings the time element is exemplified: they are filled with nostalgia for the past.

It is the haunting quality of this elaborate work which has led me to include it in this category. Incidentally, ruins were a favorite subject of the Gothic artists.

185. **Eric Freifeld**
Pig Barn, 1970–72. Pencil, 40 x 26 ins (101.6 x 66.4 cm). Collection: the artist.

Richard Robertson
1948–

Like the Freifeld (Pl. 185), this drawing induces romantic speculation. It does not appear that this deserted room was abandoned by its inhabitants in any normal circumstance. There hovers about it an aura of tragic termination.

186. Richard Robertson
The Chair, 1978. Pencil, 38½ x 43 ins (97.8 x 109.2 cm). Collection: the artist, courtesy The Prince Arthur Galleries, Toronto.

Realism: Metaphysical

John Chambers
1931–1978

One cannot look at a drawing or painting by Chambers without speculating as to its deeper levels of meaning. In him Realism is joined to Symbolism.

In our drawing, for instance, we are conscious of an exact moment in time in which some remark is being exchanged between the woman and boy, but we are also led to wonder about the significance of the whole scene in relation to our own total life experience. In this respect Chambers has links with the early nineteenth century Romantics.

187. John Chambers
Olga Along the Thames, 1963. Pen and ink,
10⁵/₁₆ x 18½ ins (26.2 x 47 cm). Collection: The
National Gallery of Canada.

Ernest Lindner
1897–

Lindner's drawings of trees in decay, although seemingly microscopically truthful to the physical appearance of the subject, are, in fact, as eloquent as those of Emily Carr. But while Carr used trees as a means of evoking worship, Lindner employs them as visual metaphors of death and renewal, no less potent for being so realistically described.

188. **Ernest Lindner**
End and Beginning, 1973. Pen and ink, 29¾ x 21⅜ ins (75.5 x 54.3 cm). Collection: The National Gallery of Canada.

Brian Kipping
1953–

This drawing stems from studies Kipping made in the palaeontology department at the Royal Ontario Museum.

Noted on the mat are the following words: "Deteriorating Image, theoretically objects tend to become colder and pale—as they become more distant. Memory/Image Invisible to Naked Eye/Evolving Image." From this inscription one can glimpse his metaphysical bent. As noted by Emerson, this leeching out of the image occurs also to the persona of great men of the past.

Kipping went on to compose "landscapes before photography," calling upon his subconscious to conjure up a primordial scenario.

189. Brian Kipping
Artifact for Gallery X, 1979. Graphite, 17 x 22 ins (43.2 x 55.9 cm). Collection: the artist, courtesy The Bau-Xi Gallery, Toronto.

New Realism

Joseph Devellano
1945–

This image is certainly candid enough, and qualifies as an example of New Realism. However, one might suggest that without the latitude established by Pop Art Devellano might not have presented horse and rider in rear view, nor have been so engaged by the numbers on his shirt.

190. **Joseph Devellano**
115, 1978. Graphite, 27 x 18 ins (68.6 x 45.7 cm). Collection: the artist, courtesy The Aggregation Gallery, Toronto.

Gary Olson
1946–

Coming under the scrutiny of the New Realists were individuals as well as groups depicting common types (often in three-dimensions). These portraits, which could be characterized as "warts and all," were sometimes in large scale, like those of Chuck Close.

    To get the full impact of this Olson portrait of his friend, the reader should visualize it as being more than three feet wide.

191. Gary Olson
Big Dick, 1976. Graphite, 30 x 40 ins (76.2 x 101.6 cm). Collection: the artist, courtesy The Aggregation Gallery, Toronto.

The Artist and the Camera

Since its invention the camera has provided artists with a third eye, offering fresh vision. Photography can freeze movement, simplify or dramatize tone through light, juggle space, explore textures and change focal perception of space. It has also been used extensively as a tool for note making.

The photographic print itself has been incorporated into assemblages and prints, and the camera's uncompromising stare has inspired original works.

D. P. Brown
1939–

Brown's drawing is an excellent example of an original work combining both the character of the photograph, which is its subject, and the vitalizing effect of the artist's vision.

192. D. P. Brown
Still Life of Old Photograph, 1973. Brush and colored inks, 26 x 36 ins (66 x 91.4 cm). Collection: Dr. Walter Stryker.

John Kerr
1955–

In Kerr's drawing the photographic source is again evident.

As with the other depictive drawings in this book, I am not offering any interpretation. However, there does appear to be an obvious contrast between the lassitude of the figure on the right with the anxiety suggested by the fragmented figure on the left.

What is extraordinary is the accomplished technique achieved by some of the New Realists.

193. John Kerr
Servant and Mistress, 1979. Pencil, 15 x 20 ins (38.1 x 50.8 cm). Collection: the artist, courtesy The Moos Gallery, Toronto.

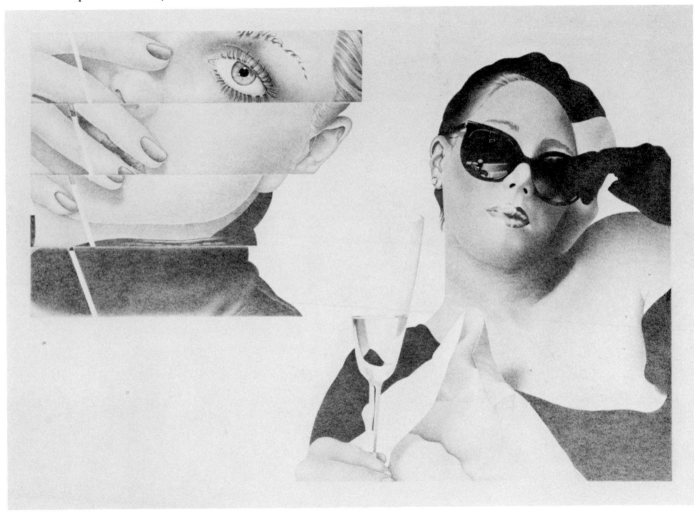

Literary Sources

The use of literature as a source of subject matter is almost as old as art itself. Artists have not only made paintings in specific illustration of various texts going back into antiquity, they have also produced independent works inspired by the characters and stories created by writers, which have become part of the myths and legends stimulating the imagination of all artists, including painters and musicians.

George Hawken
1946–

The inspiration for Hawken's drawing comes from Baudelaire's poem of the same title. Baudelaire, the first of the Symbolist poets, emphasized the dual nature of beauty and corruption.

    In style this fine drawing resembles the work of other expressionist draughtsmen such as Rico Lebrun and Leonard Baskin.

194. George Hawken
Delphine et Hippolyte, 1976. Ink, 26 x 24 ins (66 x 61 cm). Collection: the artist, courtesy The Aggregation Gallery, Toronto.

John Gould
1929–

Don Quixote has become so much a part of the collective consciousness that a new word, quixotic, was needed to define accurately the human characteristic implied in his character.

Gould's drawing expresses well the elements of tragedy and irrationality which underlie the beatific obsessions of Cervantes' hero.

195. John Gould
Don Quixote in Armour, 1975. Black and white conté, 37 x 25 ins (94 x 63.5 cm). Private collection, Detroit.

Homage to Eros

Throughout art history the human, particularly the nude, figure has been used by artists for expressive purposes. It is inevitable that the depiction of the nude should often stir feelings of sensuality inherent in our nature. Beyond that, many artists have produced works which are either subtly or frankly erotic. If a defense of such works be required, as has often been the case, it should be made on the ground that any part of human experience is a legitimate subject for artists.

I cannot resist the temptation to publish here the amusing reaction of Kenneth Clark to a copy of my book *The Nude in Canadian Painting*, which I sent him in appreciation of his magnificent book *The Nude*. He said that it came as a complete surprise to him, as he had been under the impression that Canadian art only concerned itself with "autumn tints." So much for the exposure our artists have received beyond our borders!

Bernard Mulaire
1945–

Here again is a version of the artist and model relationship (see Pls. 139, 140), this time with more overt sexual implications. Readers may make their own interpretation of the symbolism incorporated in this accomplished drawing. It has a certain Surrealist quality, as if of a dream recalled.

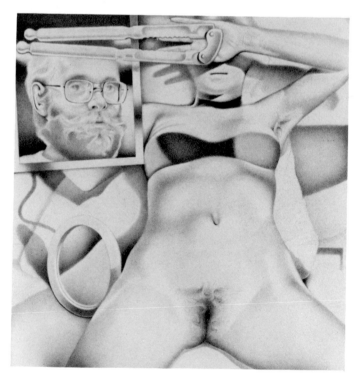

196. Bernard Mulaire
Self Portrait with Model, 1979. Pencil, 10½ x 10 ins (26.7 x 25.4 cm). Collection: the artist, courtesy The Moos Gallery, Toronto.

Graham Coughtry
1931–

The relationship of two figures has been one of
the most persistent subjects of Coughtry's paintings.

    This group of drawings is one of the finest
studies for the subject. It is not only charged
with emotion, but also monumental in form.

197. Graham Coughtry
Four Sketches for Two Figure Series, 1965. Pencil,
13⅜ x 11½ ins (34 x 29 cm). Collection: the artist,
courtesy The Isaacs Gallery, Toronto.

John Newman
1933–

Newman's drawing is one of a series of studies of young girls at the age of puberty. Evidently his purpose was to capture the complex emotional character of this life stage. Nevertheless, inevitably, an erotic element makes itself apparent, not unconnected with the role-model of Lolita.

198. John Newman
Nude about to move, 1978. Graphite and pastel, 36 x 20 ins (91.4 x 50.8 cm). Collection: the artist, courtesy The Prince Arthur Galleries, Toronto.

Harold Town
1924–

Town's love drawings are some of the most beautiful ever produced. They first appeared in the book *Love Where the Nights Are Long*, an anthology of Canadian love poems selected by Irving Layton, published by McClelland and Stewart in 1962.

The drawing below finds its way into this section only by reason of its title. It is one of a series he made which sound a distant echo of the erotic fantasies of our forbears. From their wallets he extracted a rich reward.

199. Harold Town
French Postcard, 1977. Pencil, 20¼ x 16½ ins (51.4 x 41.9 cm). Collection: the artist.

Conceptual Art

Michael Snow
1929–

Most works of art embody some concept. How are we then to define Conceptual Art? Of all too many of its manifestations it would be true to say that they are artless conceptions by people who have insufficient talent, or are too lazy, to be able to express their concepts in visual terms. If Conceptual Art is neither illuminating, provoking, nor witty, then it is just boring.

However, when a penetrating intelligence like that of Snow is brought to bear on a subject, such as the problems facing the contemporary figurative artist (which I mentioned under the heading of Pop Art), we can expect fruitful results.

In his Walking Woman series he created an emblem which he used to explore questions relating to form, content, media, space and environment. Indeed, she appeared in so many environments (including the streets of New York) that she became a visible equivalent of the ubiquitous Kilroy. Snow wrote: "The Walking Woman Works were an attempt to have variety."

In walking down a corridor of the Art Gallery of Ontario, I found that she had invaded the drawing collection. By means of frottage he had transformed his emblem into a delectable pencil drawing.

200. **Michael Snow**
Walking Woman, Series #4, 1963. Pencil, 10½ x 8¼ ins (26.7 x 21 cm). Collection: Art Gallery of Ontario. Gift of Sam and Ayala Zacks, 1970.

Photo Credits

Agnes Etherington Art Centre, 10, 21, 30, 97
Bau-Xi Gallery, 119
Charles Belair, 37, 58, 65, 67, 73
Canada Council Art Bank, 178
Canadian War Museum, 112
James Chambers, 126, 147, 154
Confederation Art Gallery, Charlottetown, 18, 19
Dalhousie University Art Gallery, 177
Galerie Dresdnere, 92
Jon Easton, 186
Glenbow-Alberta Institute, 4, 157
John Glover, 9, 14, 31, 32, 34, 48, 49, 52, 54 61, 64, 66, 70, 74-76, 90, 94, 96, 110, 123-4, 127-8, 130, 134, 139, 142, 144-6 149, 150, 152, 155, 158, 160-1, 165, 170-1, 179, 180, 193, 199
Mira Godard Gallery, 107, 118
Art Gallery of Hamilton, 40, 56
Jones-Morris Photography Ltd., 185
Henry Kahanek, 93, 175
London Regional Art Gallery, 43-4
Loranger Gallery, 77, 120
Macets Photo Arts, 172
McCord Museum, 1, 6, 12, 36
McMaster University, 91
McMichael Canadian Collection, 55, 60, 102

Montreal Museum of Fine Arts, 8, 15, 28, 39 47, 131, 168, 174
T. E. Moore, 129, 151, 169, 181, 191, 194, 197
Musée d'Art Contemporain, 103
National Gallery of Canada/Noel Saltmarche, 29, 45
National Gallery of Canada/H. Blohm, 50, 53, 71, 78-9, 82, 85, 87-8, 95, 98-9, 105-6, 108-9, 187-8
Art Gallery of Ontario/Ron Vickers, 42
Art Gallery of Ontario/James Chambers, 22
Art Gallery of Ontario, 23, 51, 84, 104, 111, 113, 115, 121, 132, 135, 137-8, 200
Ontario College of Art, 7, 24-27, 35, 46
Public Archives of Canada, 16-17
Musée du Québec/Luc Chartier, 2, 5, 38, 41
Musée du Québec/Neuville Bazin, 3, 62
Musée du Québec/P. Altman, 11
Peter Richardson, 159
Robert McLaughlin Art Gallery/P. W. Richardson, 114, 116
Charlotte Rosshandler, 122
Royal Ontario Museum, 20
Victor Sakuta, 125
Gabor Szilasi, 86
Art Gallery of Greater Victoria, 57
Provincial Archives, Victoria, 101

Index of Plates